UNDERSTANDING THE TIMES SERIES

A Biblical Worldview and Apologetics Curriculum for Grades 9–12

FOUNDATIONS

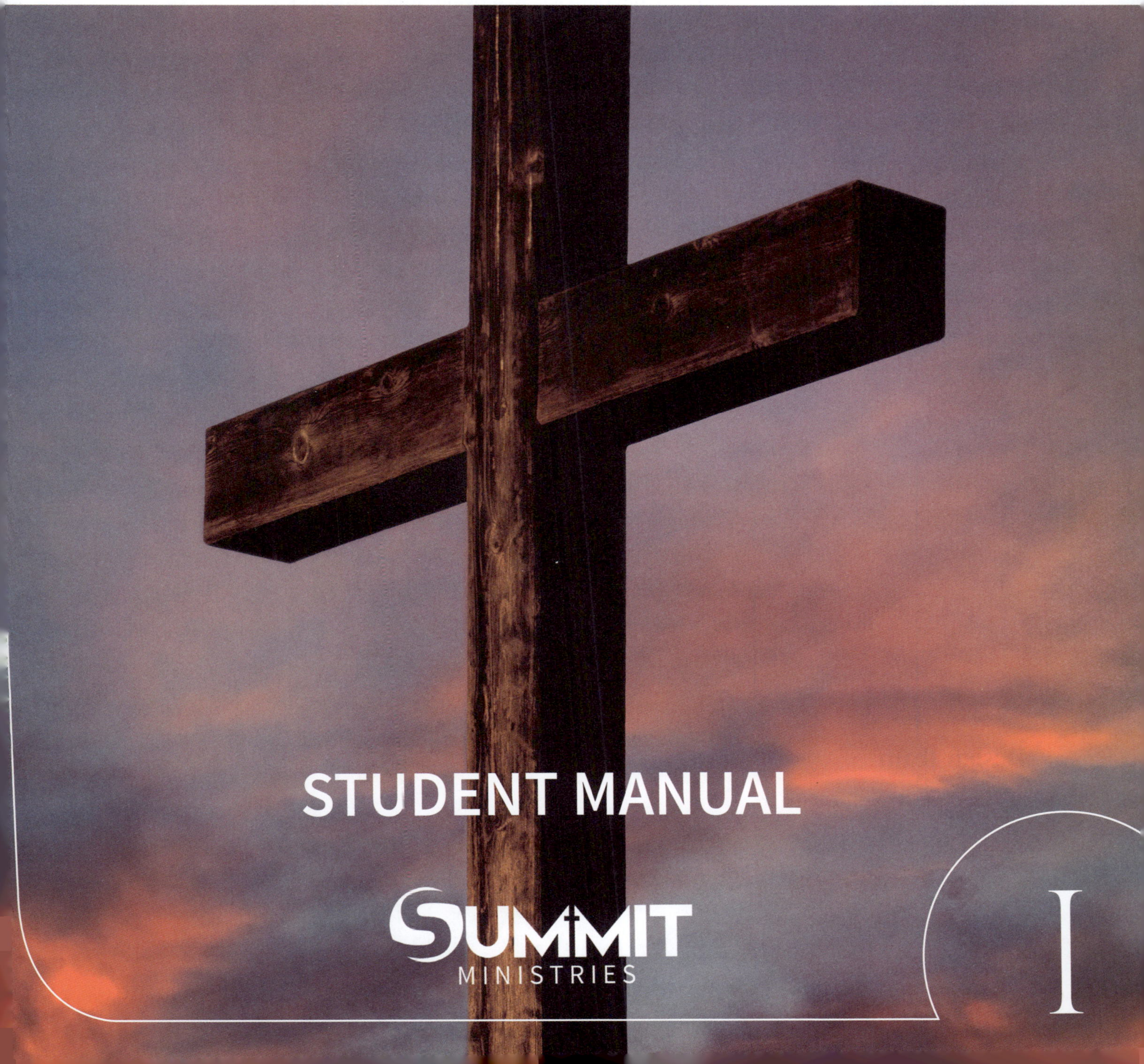

STUDENT MANUAL

SUMMIT MINISTRIES

I

Acknowledgements

Director of Publishing and Content:

Aaron Klemm

Manager of Curriculum and Instructional Design:

Macki Jones, MA Curriculum & Instruction

Authors

Ben Keiser, MATS Biblical Studies

Julie Smyth, MA Biblical Studies

Kim Pettit, MA Communications

Macki Jones, MA Curriculum & Instruction

Mike Hamel

Robin Dembicki, MEd Educational Leadership

Editorial Team

Avrie Roberts

Beth Robinson

John Conaway

Julie Smyth, MA Biblical Studies

Kim Pettit, MA Communications

Lorraine Wadman

Macki Jones, MA Curriculum & Instruction

Robin Dembicki, MEd Educational Leadership

Sabrina-Page Bernardi, MLIS

Design Team

Peter A. Schmidt

Scot McDonald

Claire Coleman

Mike Riester

Foundations, Book I of the Understanding the Times Series
Student Manual

Published by Summit Ministries
P.O. Box 207
Manitou Springs, CO 80829

ISBN: 978-1-957406-37-4

Printed in India
First Printing, 2024

Table of Contents

1

Introduction

Introduction

Chapter 1 Syllabus

Lesson		Assignment		Page
1	In Class	READ	Chapter 1.1–1.2	ST 4–7
	In Class	DISCUSS	Questions for Chapter 1.1–1.2	6–7
	In Class	EXPLORE	Activity: Curious About . . .	7
	At Home	READ	Chapter 1.3–1.4	ST 7–9
	At Home	ANSWER	Questions for Chapter 1.3–1.4	8–9
2	In Class	DISCUSS	Questions for Chapter 1.3–1.4	
	In Class	EXPLORE	Activity: Bible Scavenger Hunt	9
	At Home	READ	Chapter 1.5–1.6	ST 9–11
	At Home	ANSWER	Questions for Chapter 1.5–1.6	10–11
3	In Class	DISCUSS	Questions for Chapter 1.5–1.6	
	In Class	EXPLORE	Activity: Producer's List	11
	At Home	READ	Chapter 1.7–1.8	ST 12–13
	At Home	ANSWER	Questions for Chapter 1.7–1.8	12–13
4	In Class	DISCUSS	Questions for Chapter 1.7–1.8	
	In Class	EXPLORE	Activity: Beliefs and Behavior Brainstorm	13
	At Home	READ	Chapter 1.9–1.10	ST 14–16
	At Home	ANSWER	Questions for Chapter 1.9–1.10	14–15
5	In Class	DISCUSS	Questions for Chapter 1.9–1.10	
	In Class	EXPLORE	Activity: Being a Christian	15
6	In Class	EXPLORE	Activity: Mapmaking	
7	In Class	WATCH	Videos	
	In Class	ANSWER	Video Questions	16–18
	In Class	DISCUSS	Video Questions	
8	In Class	EXPLORE	Activity: Quiz Cards	19
	In Class	REVIEW FOR	Chapter 1 Test	20
9	In Class	STUDY FOR	Chapter 1 Test	
	In Class	ANSWER	Study Guide Questions	21–23
10	In Class	GIVE	Chapter 1 Test	
	At Home	READ	Chapter 2.1–2.2	ST 17–20
	At Home	ANSWER	Questions for Chapter 2.1–2.2	26

*Student Textbook (ST) Student Manual (SM)

CH 1

Chapter 1.1–1.2

DISCUSSION QUESTIONS

1. How do people find directions for life and answers to life's biggest questions? [1.1]

2. What is a worldview? [1.1]

3. How would you describe your worldview? [1.1]

4. Before reading Chapter 1.2, what did you think being a Christian meant? Can you relate to any of the three misconceptions discussed there? Explain. [1.2]

5. What does it mean to be a Christian according to the Bible? [1.2]

6. What does Chapter 1.2 say that Christians believe about Jesus? [1.2]

Activity

CURIOUS ABOUT . . .

OBJECTIVE:
You will express, expand, and clarify your personal ideas about Jesus, Christianity, the Bible, and worldview.

PREPARATION:
- Materials needed: index cards and pen
- Time required: 10–15 minutes

PROCEDURE:
1. Reflect on the ideas shared in the class discussion questions.
2. On the index card provided, write a brief response to the following question: "What is something from our class discussion that stirred your curiosity?" Your response can be about Jesus, Christianity, the Bible, or worldview.
3. When you have finished writing, turn your index card over and write a brief response to the following question: "What is something you would like to or hope to learn more about in this class?"
4. If time permits, find a partner and share your responses with each other.
5. You may keep your card or turn it in to the teacher for review on the last day of class.

CH 1 Chapter 1.3–1.4

DISCUSSION QUESTIONS

1. What is the Bible? How would you describe it in your own words? [1.3]

2. Do you think that an idea should be dismissed simply because it is old? Why or why not? [1.3]

3. What is proof texting, and how can this Bible-reading mistake be avoided? [1.4]

4. Why is it a mistake to make pursuing the Bible our end goal? [1.4]

5. What does it mean to call the Bible a story? How do you react to the idea that the Bible is a story? [1.4]

Activity

BIBLE SCAVENGER HUNT

OBJECTIVE:

You will use your Bible to find the answers to Bible-related questions.

PREPARATION:

- Materials needed: TR 1.2A, Bible, and pen
- Time required: 15–20 minutes

PROCEDURE:

1. Your teacher will divide the class into groups.
2. Decide on a name for your group and write it at the top of TR 1.2A Bible Scavenger Hunt. Your group will race against the others to complete the scavenger hunt. Assign each member of the group to work on specific questions and look up the answers in your Bibles.
3. After the race, mark your correct answers as your teacher gives them. The group that has answered the most questions correctly wins. If groups are tied, the group that finished first wins.

CH 1

Chapter 1.5–1.6

DISCUSSION QUESTIONS

1. What has been your experience of reading the Bible? Do you find it uplifting? Encouraging? Confusing? Frustrating? Something else? Explain. [1.5]

2. Describe what happened in the first two acts of the biblical story. [1.5]

3. Describe what happened in the third act and interlude of the biblical story. [1.5]

4. In what act of the biblical story did Jesus appear? Who was he, and what did he do? [1.6]

5. Describe what happened in Act 5: Restoration Initiated. [1.6]

6. What will happen in Act 6: Restoration Accomplished? How does the grand story of Scripture end? [1.6]

Activity

PRODUCER'S LIST

OBJECTIVE:

You will associate items related to the acts of the biblical story.

PREPARATION:

- Materials needed: die or dice
- Time required: 20–25 minutes

PROCEDURE:

1. Your teacher will write the number and name of the six acts on the board.
2. Sit in a circle with your classmates as assigned. Your teacher will choose a student to begin the activity and give him or her the die.
3. That student will roll the die and say, "I am the producer of a Bible drama." The number rolled will determine which act he or she will use in the next sentence: "In my show, for Act ____, I will need ____." To complete the second part of the sentence, the student should name an object, person, or concept related to the act. For example, "I am the producer of a Bible drama. In my show, for Act 2, I need an apple."
4. The next student to play is the one on the right of the first student. Students will take turns around the circle. Each subsequent person repeats what was stated by the previous person, rolls the die, and adds an additional act and item. For example, "I am the producer of a Bible drama. In my show, for Act 2, I need an apple. For Act 1, I need darkness" and so on.
5. If a student makes a mistake on an act or an item, that student is out of the game.
6. The game will continue as long as desired or until there is only one player left in the circle.

CH 1 Chapter 1.7–1.8

DISCUSSION QUESTIONS

1. Why do you think Proverbs 9:10 says, "The fear of the LORD is the beginning of wisdom, and the knowledge of the Holy One is insight"? [1.7]

2. When you think about God, what comes to mind? What is God like? [1.7]

3. What do you think it means that God is called *the Trinity*? [1.7]

4. Think about where you find your identity. What makes you who you are? [1.7]

5. How does our behavior influence our beliefs? [1.8]

6. Why do Christians teach that pornography is wrong? [1.8]

7. Why do Christians engage in spiritual disciplines? [1.8]

Activity

BELIEFS AND BEHAVIOR BRAINSTORM

OBJECTIVE:

You will assess how beliefs affect behavior and how behavior affects beliefs.

PREPARATION:

- Materials needed: none
- Time required: 15–20 minutes

PROCEDURE:

1. Your teacher will draw a T-chart on the board. The left side will have the heading Beliefs Affect Behavior; the right side, Behavior Affects Beliefs.
2. Discuss the two examples your teacher shows you.
3. Brainstorm other examples for each side of the chart, starting with the left side and then working on the right side.

CH 1

Chapter 1.9–1.10

DISCUSSION QUESTIONS

1. Imagine for a moment that you are not a Christian. What do you think would make it difficult for you to become a Christian? What would bother you about Christianity? [1.9]

2. Why shouldn't Christianity be judged solely by our experiences with Christians? [1.9]

3. Some people think that loving others requires that you accept whatever they do as right and even good for them. Do you believe this? Why or why not? [1.9]

4. How would you describe God's love for us and the love that Christians are called to demonstrate? [1.9]

5. Your textbook says that it is written from a Protestant perspective. What do you understand this to mean? [1.10]

6. Chapter 1.10 offers four suggestions for beginning the journey through this book. The first of these is to "think about where you are in relationship to the Christian faith." How would you respond to that statement? [1.10]

Activity

BEING A CHRISTIAN

OBJECTIVE:

You will discuss quotations about being a Christian and relate them to the misconceptions described in the textbook.

PREPARATION:

- Materials needed: TR 1.5A
- Time required: 15–20 minutes

PROCEDURE:

1. Work with a partner.
2. Read TR 1.5A Being a Christian, discuss the quotations, and relate them to the misconceptions described in Chapter 1.2.
3. Be ready to share your reactions with the class.

CH 1

Videos

DISCUSSION QUESTIONS

Read the discussion questions before each video is played so that you know what to listen for.

Video 1: What Is a Worldview, and Why Does It Matter?

1. How does the speaker describe what a worldview is?

2. How do ideas about God and reality impact morals and behaviors?

3. What is one of the most important things that Christians can do with worldview patterns?

Video 2: How Can Christians Become More Intentional about Their Worldview?

1. How is secularism most powerful in its challenges to faith?

2. In what ways have Christians adopted a worldview of secularism?

3. How should we view and talk about faith?

Video 3: How Should We Begin Studying Worldview?

1. How can you decide what apologetics resources to read?

2. What is the best way to learn worldview?

3. How can you avoid being overwhelmed by the resources out there?

Video 4: Is Christianity Just a List of Rules to Follow?

1. What suspicion did the speaker say he had when he was younger? Do you agree or disagree with that suspicion? Why or why not?

2. What does the speaker say about whether Christianity is a religion or a relationship?

3. What does the speaker say makes Christianity different from other religions and philosophies?

4. What problems and questions are answered in or through Jesus?

Video 5: How Can We Overcome Apathy towards Christianity?

1. What worldviews does the speaker say competed with Christianity where he grew up? How did he describe them?

2. To counter apathy, the speaker recommended two why questions for every what in a conversation. Explain what he meant.

CH 1

Videos (continued)

3. What two things did the speaker say people are interested in that Christianity provides answers to?

Video 6: How Can Christians Portray the Fulfilling Life Jesus Gives?

1. What misconception do people often have about the gospel? Why is it wrong?

2. The speaker said that the gospel "summons us to participate in a story where we are no longer the star of our own story but find significance outside of ourselves." What is your reaction to this statement?

3. Why does the speaker mention morality, culture, beauty, truth, goodness, and justice?

Activity

QUIZ CARDS

OBJECTIVE

You will review the chapter by formulating questions to quiz your classmates.

PREPARATION:

- Materials needed: index cards, student textbook, and pen
- Time required: 20–30 minutes

PROCEDURE:

1. Your teacher will tell you to write a total of nine questions—one question for each section from Chapter 1.1–1.9. Use the index cards you received to write three quiz questions per card and then write the answers for those questions on the back. You may use the textbook in drafting your questions but not the student manual.
2. You will have up to 15 minutes to write your questions and the answers.
3. Choose a partner and quiz each other. Then change partners and repeat the process.

CH 1

Chapter 1 Review

Take notes during the slide presentation.

Chapter 1 Study Guide

Key Terms
worldview
Christian

Key Verses
Luke 18:22
Proverbs 9:10

1. How is a worldview like a map? Give examples of some worldviews.

2. Explain why it is wrong to say that to be a Christian you have to meet one of three conditions: you must be born into a Christian family, you must follow certain rules, or you must focus only on heaven.

3. What do Christians believe about Jesus?

4. Why is the Bible important to and authoritative for Christians even though it is such an old book?

5. Describe the Bible. What is it? How is it organized?

6. What are two mistakes that people make in reading the Bible?

CH 1 Study Guide *(continued)*

7. What are the first three acts of the biblical story, and where are they found in the Bible? What is the interlude? Describe the acts and the interlude.

8. What are the three final acts of the biblical story? Where are they found in the Bible? Describe them.

9. Theology is the study of God. Anthropology is the study of human beings. Why should we know God and know ourselves?

10. Why is becoming like Christ a lifelong process? What helps us to become like him?

11. What is a Christian's primary calling? Why?

12. Why are there Christians who are sinful or judgmental?

13. What four things does your student textbook invite you to do in the conclusion to Chapter 1?

14. Why does your student textbook promote the Christian worldview?

15. Why does so much of the Bible focus on the story of the nation of Israel? Why is Israel important?

16. What does it mean to say that the church lives in *an already, not yet* time?

17. Read and study the two Key Verses listed at the top of the study guide.

2

What the Bible Is and Isn't

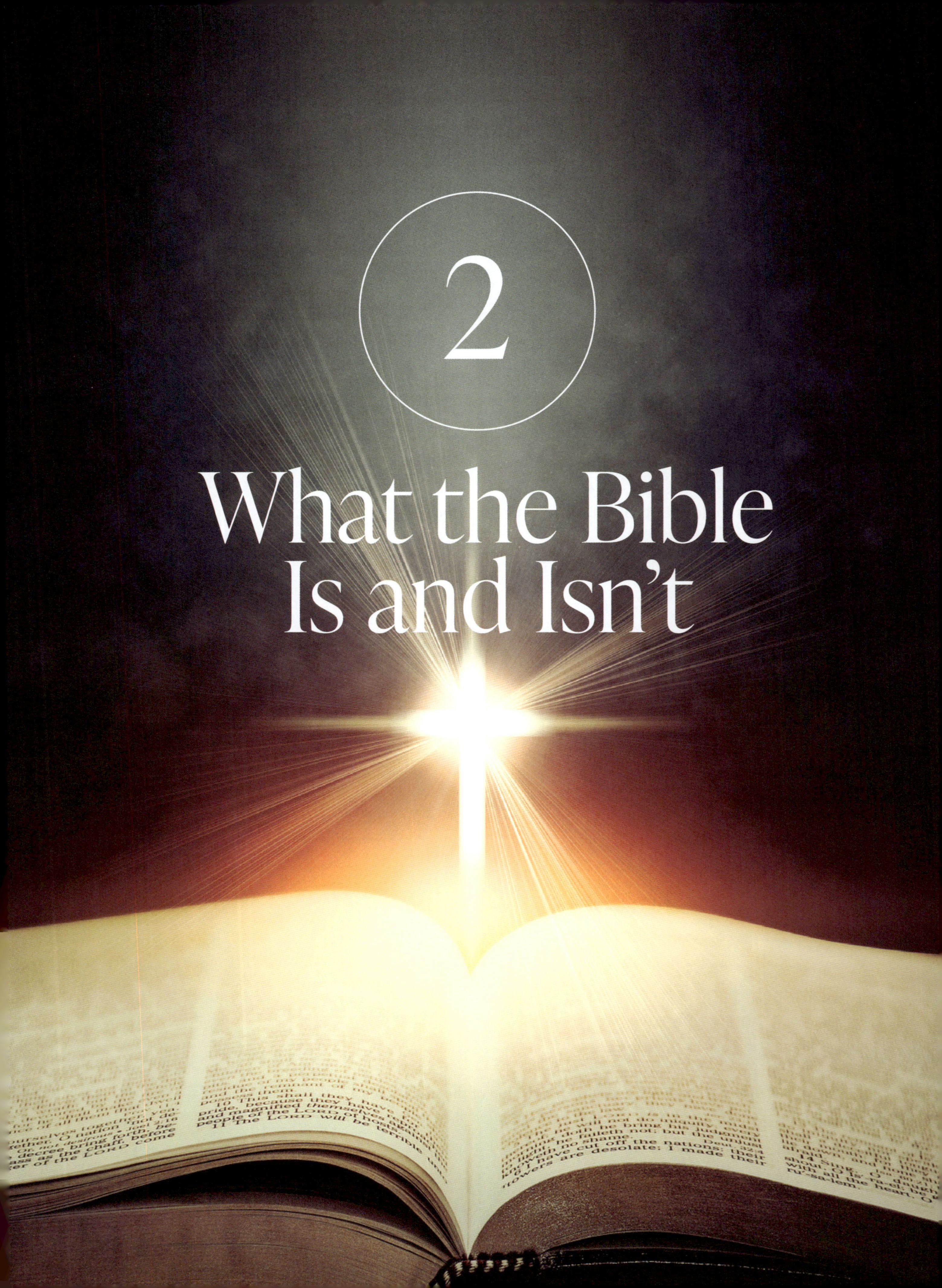

What the Bible Is and Isn't

Chapter 2 Syllabus

Lesson		Assignment		Page
1	In Class	REVIEW	Chapter 1 Test	
	In Class	DISCUSS	Questions for Chapter 2.1–2.2	26
	In Class	EXPLORE	Activity: What Do You Know?	27
	At Home	READ	Chapter 2.3–2.4	ST 20–22
	At Home	ANSWER	Questions for Chapter 2.3–2.4	28–29
2	In Class	DISCUSS	Questions for Chapter 2.3–2.4	
	In Class	EXPLORE	Activity: Not Just a Book of Instructions	29
	At Home	READ	Chapter 2.5–2.6	ST 23–25
	At Home	ANSWER	Questions for Chapter 2.5–2.6	30–31
3	In Class	DISCUSS	Questions for Chapter 2.5–2.6	
	In Class	EXPLORE	Activity: God's Revelation	31
	At Home	READ	Chapter 2.7–2.8	ST 25–28
	At Home	ANSWER	Questions for Chapter 2.7–2.8	32–33
4	In Class	DISCUSS	Questions for Chapter 2.7–2.8	
	In Class	EXPLORE	Activity: The Bible Is Rooted in History	33
	At Home	READ	Chapter 2.9–2.10	ST 28–30
	At Home	ANSWER	Questions for Chapter 2.9–2.10	34
5	In Class	DISCUSS	Questions for Chapter 2.9–2.10	
	In Class	EXPLORE	Activity: Why Truth Matters	35
6	In Class	EXPLORE	Activity: Two Truths and One Opinion	
7	In Class	WATCH	Videos	
	In Class	ANSWER	Video Questions	36–38
	In Class	DISCUSS	Video Questions	
8	In Class	EXPLORE	Activity: The Bible Is the Word of God	39
	In Class	REVIEW FOR	Chapter 2 Test	40
9	In Class	STUDY FOR	Chapter 2 Test	
	In Class	ANSWER	Study Guide Questions	41–43
10	In Class	GIVE	Chapter 2 Test	
	At Home	READ	Chapter 3.1–3.2	ST 31–34
	At Home	ANSWER	Questions for Chapter 3.1–3.2	46

*Student Textbook (ST) Student Manual (SM)

CH 2

Chapter 2.1–2.2

DISCUSSION QUESTIONS

1. List and describe the four ways in which the Bible has influenced the world. [2.1]

2. Explain four common ways people approach and read the Bible. [2.2]

3. Which of the four approaches do you currently use when reading the Bible? Explain. [2.2]

4. Have you ever changed your approach to studying the Bible? How? [2.2]

Activity

WHAT DO YOU KNOW?

OBJECTIVE:

You will assess your knowledge of the Bible and compare your results to those of surveys conducted in the United States.

PREPARATION:

- Materials Needed: paper and pen
- Time required: 15–20 minutes

PROCEDURE:

1. In the space below, write your answers to the following Bible questions:
   - Name the first five books of the Bible in the proper order.
   - Name the four Gospels.
   - Yes or no, is the Bible the literal and inspired Word of God?
2. Check your paper as your teacher reads the answers out loud.
3. Work together to calculate the class percentages of correct responses for each question. Compare your class response percentages with the results of national surveys.
4. Participate in class discussion.

CH 2

Chapter 2.3–2.4

DISCUSSION QUESTIONS

1. Describe how the Bible is arranged, and explain each component. [2.3]

2. What is the Apocrypha, and why isn't it included in all Bibles? [2.3]

3. Why is the Bible not like a rule book? [2.4]

4. How is the Bible like a map? [2.4]

5. Describe how the Bible is like a compass. [2.4]

6. How do you see the Bible—like a rule book, a to-do list, a map, a compass, or something else? Explain your answer. [2.4]

7. Why is the Bible a better compass than the books that other religions view as holy? [2.4]

Activity

NOT JUST A BOOK OF INSTRUCTIONS

OBJECTIVE:
You will write a how-to guide for using the Bible in your life.

PREPARATION:
- Materials needed: paper and pen
- Time required: 15–20 minutes

PROCEDURE:
1. Choose a partner and work together to write a how-to guide for using the Bible as an owner's manual in your life.
2. When everyone has finished, share your work with the class.
3. Discuss common themes that appeared and why.

CH 2

Chapter 2.5–2.6

DISCUSSION QUESTIONS

1. What does it mean to say that God is personal? [2.5]

2. What does *revelation* mean? [2.5]

3. What are the two ways in which God's reveals his character? Explain the difference between the two ways. Give an example of how you have experienced each one personally. [2.5]

4. What is the canon? How was the canon formed? [2.6]

5. What three criteria were used to select the books of the New Testament? What question does each criteria answer? [2.6]

Activity

GOD'S REVELATION

OBJECTIVE:

You will write down items from A–Z that reveal God's nature and character through general revelation.

PREPARATION:

- Materials needed: paper and pen
- Time required: 20–25 minutes

PROCEDURE:

1. Discuss general revelation together as a class.
2. Take a sheet of paper and write the letters of the alphabet down the side. You will have 10 minutes to write one item of creation that reveals God's nature and character for each letter of the alphabet, such as A: atom; B: baboon. You will receive one point for each item you write that no one else in the class wrote down.
3. At the end of 10 minutes, stop writing.
4. Starting with A, take turns calling out what the class wrote down. If more than one person wrote the same thing, no one scores a point.
5. Continue this process as you work through the alphabet.
6. Total your points.
7. Discuss what you learned about God from this activity.

CH 2

Chapter 2.7–2.8

DISCUSSION QUESTIONS

1. What is the difference between saying the Bible contains God's words and the Bible is God's Word? [2.7]

2. What does *inspiration* mean, and how does it relate to the Bible? [2.7]

3. Can the Bible be trusted as accurate? [2.7]

4. What does inerrancy mean, and how does it help us be confident that the Bible is God's Word? [2.7]

5. What is the correspondence theory of truth? How does it pertain to the Bible? [2.8]

Activity

THE BIBLE IS ROOTED IN HISTORY

OBJECTIVE:

You will support how the Bible is rooted in history.

PREPARATION:

- Materials needed: computer, paper, and pen
- Time required: 20–30 minutes

PROCEDURE:

1. Work individually, in pairs, or groups, depending on how many computers are available.
2. Research to find two historical facts from the Old Testament and two from the New Testament that have scientifically been proven accurate.
3. Record each historical fact, how it was proven accurate, and the website where you found the information.
4. If time permits, share some of your historical facts with the class.

CH 2

Chapter 2.9–2.10

DISCUSSION QUESTIONS

1. What is relativism? Describe why relativism is a false belief. [2.9]

2. Relativism implies there is no truth because truth is relative to the individual. Explain why the statement "There is no truth" is a self-refuting claim. [2.9]

3. Why does truth matter? [2.9]

4. What is the purpose of the Bible? [2.10]

Activity

WHY TRUTH MATTERS

OBJECTIVE:

You will give examples of relativism and evaluate whether they are objective or subjective truth claims.

PREPARATION:

- Materials needed: paper and pen
- Time required: 20–30 minutes

PROCEDURE:

1. You will need to know that an objective truth claim is a claim that does not depend on one's belief. It is based on facts. A subjective truth claim is a claim based on the idea that truth changes according to one's belief. It is based on feelings or opinions instead of facts.
2. Gather into five groups. Each group will receive a paper from their teacher.
3. Your teacher will name a topic such as cheating, stealing, or doing drugs. Your group will work together to assume the role on the paper and respond with how your character would apply relativism to the topic.
4. One group at a time will give their response and ask the other groups what the Bible says is the objective truth claim about the topic. Then explain why your topic is not a subjective truth claim.
5. Continue this process with the other four groups.

CH 2

Videos

DISCUSSION QUESTIONS

Read the discussion questions before each video is played so that you know what to listen for.

Video 1: How Did We Get the Bible?

1. Explain the first criterion discussed by the speaker that was used for determining whether a document was included in the New Testament.

2. Who were two writers of New Testament books that were not eyewitnesses? Why were their books included in the New Testament canon?

3. Early followers of Jesus, such as Ignatius, Papias, and Polycarp who were students of John, quoted from the Gospels. Irenaeus, a third-generation Christian, listed the New Testament books he used with his students. How does this help prove the reliability of the New Testament?

4. The speaker used to be a skeptic but then became a Christian because of reliable evidence. Would having eyewitness testimony about an event help make you feel more confident about its authenticity? Why or why not?

Video 2: Is the Bible Applicable?

1. What question do people generally ask when they read the Bible?

2. Is that the first question we should be asking when we read the Bible? Why or why not?

3. What two steps does the speaker recommend for reading the Bible?

4. Explain why Exodus 14:14 does not apply to us in the same way as it did for the Israelites.

5. How is Exodus 14:14 relevant to us?

Video 3: Is the Bible's Impact Important?

1. Is the Bible the only religious book that has had a major impact on the world? Is a book's impact a good final measure for evaluating its value? Why or why not?

2. What is another way to assess a book's value?

3. Compare the Quran and the Book of Mormon to the Bible. What makes the Bible unique and different from those other religious books?

CH 2

Videos (continued)

Video 4: Isn't Christianity a Bunch of Rules and Regulations?

1. What is a common concern people have about Christianity?

2. What is the problem with this concern?

3. Do your parents have rules and expectations for you? What are some of them? Why do you think your parents have those rules and expectations?

4. How is the relationship between children and their parents far more than following a bunch of rules?

5. How would you explain to someone that Christianity, God, and the Bible are not just a bunch of rules and regulations we are required to follow?

Activity

THE BIBLE IS THE WORD OF GOD

OBJECTIVE

You will defend that the Bible is truth and the Word of God.

PREPARATION:

- Materials needed: student textbook and pen
- Time required: 20–30 minutes

PROCEDURE:

1. Your group will be assigned one of the topics from the student textbook. Put a check by the topic assigned :
   - The Importance of the Bible in History
   - Not Merely a Book of Instructions
   - What Does It Mean to Call the Bible "Revelation"?
   - How We Got the Bible
   - What Does It Mean to Say the Bible Is the "Word of God"?
2. Find the section in your textbook that has your topic title. Review the section with your group and discuss how you would use that information to show a skeptic that the Bible is the true Word of God.
3. In the space below, write five points you can use for your defense.
4. Present your group's points to the class.
5. Listen to other groups' feedback on which of your points they feel are the most compelling.

FIVE POINTS DEFENSE:

1. ________________________________

2. ________________________________

3. ________________________________

4. ________________________________

5. ________________________________

CH 2

Chapter 2 Review

Take notes during the slide presentation.

Chapter 2 Study Guide

Key Terms
Apocrypha
general revelation
special revelation
canon
inspiration
inerrancy
relativism

Key Verses
Psalm 19:1–4
Romans 1:19–20
Romans 2:14–15
2 Timothy 3:16

1. What are four ways in which the Bible has influenced the world?

2. List and explain four ways people approach and read the Bible today.

3. Describe the different components of the Bible, and how it is arranged.

4. Explain why the Bible can be referred to as a map. How it is like a compass?

5. Explain the difference between general and special revelation.

CH 2

Study Guide *(continued)*

6. How was the canon of Scripture was formed?

7. Describe the three criteria used to select the books of the New Testament.

8. Explain why it is false to say the Bible contains God's words.

9. Give three reasons to be confident that the entire Bible is God's Word.

10. What is the correspondence theory of truth? How does it relate to the Bible?

11. Why is relativism a false belief?

12. Explain why truth matters.

13. What is the Apocrypha?

14. Distinguish between inspiration and inerrancy.

15. Read and study the four Key Verses listed at the top of the study guide.

3

Does the Bible Have Authority?

Does the Bible Have Authority?

Chapter 3 Syllabus

Lesson		Assignment		Page
1	In Class	REVIEW	Chapter 2 Test	
	In Class	DISCUSS	Questions for Chapter 3.1–3.2	46
	In Class	EXPLORE	Activity: Jesus and the Old Testament	47
	At Home	READ	Chapter 3.3–3.4	ST 34–37
	At Home	ANSWER	Questions for Chapter 3.3–3.4	48
2	In Class	DISCUSS	Questions for Chapter 3.3–3.4	
	In Class	EXPLORE	Activity: Recognize the Evidence	49
	At Home	READ	Chapter 3.5–3.6	ST 38–40
	At Home	ANSWER	Questions for Chapter 3.5–3.6	50–51
3	In Class	DISCUSS	Questions for Chapter 3.5–3.6	
	In Class	EXPLORE	Activity: How High Is the Evidence?	51
	At Home	READ	Chapter 3.7–3.8	ST 41–43
	At Home	ANSWER	Questions for Chapter 3.7–3.8	52–53
4	In Class	DISCUSS	Questions for Chapter 3.7–3.8	
	In Class	EXPLORE	Activity: Answering the Skeptic	53
	At Home	READ	Chapter 3.9–3.10	ST 44–47
	At Home	ANSWER	Questions for Chapter 3.9–3.10	54
5	In Class	DISCUSS	Questions for Chapter 3.9–3.10	
	In Class	EXPLORE	Activity: Idolatry Bible Study	55
6	In Class	EXPLORE	Activity: Recognize, Evaluate, Decide	
7	In Class	WATCH	Videos	
	In Class	ANSWER	Video Questions	56–58
	In Class	DISCUSS	Video Questions	
8	In Class	EXPLORE	Activity: Evidence Tag	59
	In Class	REVIEW FOR	Chapter 3 Test	60
9	In Class	STUDY FOR	Chapter 3 Test	
	In Class	ANSWER	Study Guide Questions	61–63
10	In Class	TAKE	Chapter 3 Test	
	At Home	READ	Chapter 4.1–4.2	ST 48–51
	At Home	ANSWER	Questions for Chapter 4.1–4.2	66–67

*Student Textbook (ST) Student Manual (SM)

CH 3

Chapter 3.1–3.2

DISCUSSION QUESTIONS

1. Is it ever okay to question authority? Why or why not? [3.1]

2. What does it mean to confess "Jesus is Lord"? [3.1]

3. How did the Old Testament authors indicate that their writings were authoritative? [3.2]

4. Why does Jesus' affirmation of the Old Testament matter? [3.2]

Activity

JESUS AND THE OLD TESTAMENT

OBJECTIVE:

You will analyze Scripture passages for truths about Jesus' support for the authority of the Old Testament.

PREPARATION:

- Materials needed: student textbook, Bible, paper, and pen
- Time required: 15–20 minutes

PROCEDURE:

1. with a partner to answer one of the following questions with its accompanying Bible verse(s). Put a checkmark by your assigned question.
   - How does Jesus confirm the divine origin of Scripture? (Mark 7:13)
   - How does Jesus show belief that Scripture is the final authority? (Matthew 15:3, 19:4–5)
   - How does Jesus demonstrate belief that the Old Testament prophecies would be fulfilled? (John 13:18 and 15:25)
   - How does Jesus confirm that Old Testament miracles were real? (Matthew 12:40)
   - How did Jesus rely on the Old Testament in times of distress? (Matthew 4:3–4, Mark 15:34)
   - How did Jesus' use of Old Testament stories demonstrate how he viewed the Old Testament? (Mark 2:25 and John 8:56)
   - How did Jesus reaffirm the Old Testament? (Matthew 5:17–20)
   - How did Jesus base his own teaching on the Old Testament? (Genesis 1:27, Mark 10:6)
   - How did Jesus indicate that Scripture is not merely human tradition? (Matthew 15:3)
   - How did Jesus build on the foundation of the Old Testament? (Matthew 5:27–28)
2. Read your assigned verses and discuss the question. Write the answer on your paper.
3. Be prepared to present your answer to the class. Use the list in Chapter 3.2 of your student textbook as a guideline for checking answers.

CH 3

Chapter 3.3–3.4

DISCUSSION QUESTIONS

1. In what ways did the New Testament writers talk about the authority of their writings? [3.3]

2. Does the internal evidence for the authority of Scripture prove anything? Why or why not? [3.3]

3. How do historical and archeological discoveries support the reliability of the Old Testament? [3.4]

4. What role does fulfilled prophecy play in supporting the reliability of the Old Testament? [3.4]

Activity

RECOGNIZE THE EVIDENCE

OBJECTIVE:

You will create memory aids to help you recall specific evidence for the reliability of the Old Testament.

PREPARATION:

- Materials needed: poster board and markers
- Time required: 20–25 minutes

PROCEDURE:

1. Work with your group. Obtain one posterboard and several markers. Your teacher will assign you one of the following categories: (1) historical events confirmed by extra-biblical sources, (2) archaeological discoveries, or (3) fulfillment of prophecies.
2. Brainstorm and design symbols, acronyms, rhymes, or visual cues that can help you memorize two to four examples of non-biblical evidence affirming the reliability of the Old Testament.
3. Present your memory aids to the class.

CH 3

Chapter 3.5–3.6

DISCUSSION QUESTIONS

1. What ancient non-Christian writings mention Jesus and the basic teachings of the early Christians? Why are these sources important? [3.5]

2. How do historical and archeological discoveries support the reliability of the New Testament? [3.5]

3. How important is external evidence in supporting the reliability of Scripture? [3.5]

4. What evidence is there that the Old Testament has been accurately preserved? [3.6]

5. What evidence supports the notion that the New Testament has been accurately preserved? [3.6]

Activity

HOW HIGH IS THE EVIDENCE?

OBJECTIVE:

You will compare the available New Testament manuscripts with the available manuscripts of other ancient documents.

PREPARATION:

- Materials needed: calculator, ruler, computer (optional), paper, and pencil
- Time required: 15–20 minutes

PROCEDURE:

1. At your teacher's cue, if you are over five feet five inches tall, give a thumbs up and tell your height. If you are less than five feet five inches, give the "v for victory" sign and tell your height when your teacher asks. Write down everyone's height on a piece of paper.
2. Add up all the heights. Write the total combined heights in feet and inches.
3. Work with a partner to create a bar graph showing the students' total height, the height of stacked New Testament manuscripts, and the average stack of other ancient non-biblical manuscript collections. (If a computer is available, you may add more bars to your graph by researching specific numbers of manuscripts for other ancient documents, such as Homer's *Iliad*, or other frames of reference, such as the height of the Empire State Building for comparison).
4. Use this information to create your bar graph: As of 2017, the total number of early New Testament manuscripts in Greek was over 5,800. Early non-Greek manuscripts totaled over 18,130. The total of all those early manuscripts amounts to more than 23,930 manuscripts. If all these manuscripts were stacked, they would be over a mile high. Stacks of existing manuscripts from other ancient books average four feet high.

CH 3

Chapter 3.7–3.8

DISCUSSION QUESTIONS

1. How could you respond to someone who says the Bible is just another human book written by fallible people? [3.7]

2. How could you respond to someone who says the Bible has been corrupted over time? [3.7]

3. How could you respond to someone who says that important books have been excluded from the Bible? [3.7]

4. How is gnosticism different from Christianity? [3.7]

5. How far does God's authority extend? [3.8]

Activity

ANSWERING THE SKEPTIC

OBJECTIVE:

You will respond to common objections to the authority of the Bible.

PREPARATION:

- Materials needed: index cards with prewritten sentences, container, and pen
- Time required: 20–25 minutes

PROCEDURE:

1. Work with a partner. One of you will act as a skeptic, and the other will respond as the Christian.
2. One student in each pair will draw a card from the container. The student with the card will be the skeptic and cannot show the card to the other student.
3. The skeptic starts a brief conversation about Christianity or the Bible with the student playing the role of the Christian. During the conversation, the skeptic must bring up the objection on the card drawn from the container in the skeptic's own words. The Christian should respond conversationally by using the information they have learned in the lesson. Remember to ask respectful questions for clarity, such as variations of "What do you mean by _____?" or "How did you come to that conclusion?" can help them make sure they are answering the correct objection.
4. Once you finish the initial role play, put the card back into the container. Then switch roles. The new skeptic will draw a different objection card. Repeat the activity.

CH 3

Chapter 3.9–3.10

DISCUSSION QUESTIONS

1. What if an authority figure in your life makes a mistake or is wrong about something—does that give you the right to ignore or disobey him or her? Why or why not? [3.9]

2. How should Christians question authority? [3.9]

3. How does God use his authority? [3.9]

4. Why does submitting to authority require faith? Is this blind faith? [3.10]

Activity

IDOLATRY BIBLE STUDY

OBJECTIVE:

You will analyze verses about idolatry and explain how they apply to pecple today.

PREPARATION:

- Materials needed: TR 3.5A, Bible, and pen
- Time required: 20–25 minutes

PROCEDURE:

1. Obtain a copy of TR 3.5A Idolatry Bible Study from your teacher.
2. Read the instructions and complete the activity individually.
3. Share your answers with the class.
4. If time permits, discuss the questions below:
   - Which step—recognize, evalute, or decide—did you find most helpful? Explain.
   - What were your initial thoughts when you read Exodus 20:1–6?
   - How does Romans 1:18–20 relate to Exodus 20:1–6?
   - Do you think it is possible to make an idol out of yourself? How?
   - God should always be our provider, protector, and source of power. Are there any ways in which you have attempted to do God's job? For example, have you ever tried to make something happen the way you wanted it to go?

CH 3

Videos

DISCUSSION QUESTIONS

Read the discussion questions before each video is played so that you know what to listen for.

Video 1: Why Does Our Faith Need Evidence?

1. Why do some people walk away from Christianity temporarily or permanently?

2. What is a strong alternative to blind faith?

3. What does developing forensic faith do for us?

Video 2: Is It Possible to Make a Case for Christianity without the Bible?

1. Can the case for a creator be made without the Bible? Explain.

2. Does the evidence of design in biology and the fine-tuning of the universe make a compelling case for Christianity? Why or why not?

3. What is the key evidence for the truth of Christianity, and how does it relate to the eyewitness accounts in the Gospels?

Video 3: What Makes Eyewitness Testimony Important?

1. What is a key difference between Christianity and other theistic worldviews?

2. Why are eyewitness accounts important?

3. What writings were used by early Christians? What was the criteria for including writings in the New Testament canon?

Video 4: How Was the New Testament Created?

1. How was the New Testament created?

2. Explain the relationship between the eyewitnesses and the students whose work confirms most of the New Testament canon.

3. Was the first New Testament canon formed and put into use before, during, or after the earliest church councils?

4. What role did the church councils play?

5. What three criteria did the church councils use to evaluate false ideas and documents about Jesus?

CH 3

Videos *(continued)*

Video 5: Can We Rely on the Disciples' Words in the Gospels?

1. Does the fact that the Gospels were written by Christians hurt their credibility as the testimony of eyewitnesses? Why or why not?

2. What are the four tests used by detectives to determine if an eyewitness can be trusted?

Video 6: Don't the Gospels Contradict? (optional)

1. Why should we consider the Gospel accounts as eyewitness testimony?

2. Why are there differences between eyewitness accounts of an event?

3. Should we trust the testimony of eyewitnesses more when they match perfectly or when they contain variances?

Activity

EVIDENCE TAG

OBJECTIVE:

You will identify and categorize specific evidence as either internal or external evidence for the reliability of Scripture.

PREPARATION:

- Materials needed: TRs 3.8A–B, masking tape, and a soft object to toss
- Time required: 20–25 minutes

PROCEDURE:

1. Take an "evidence tag" from TRs 3.8A–B Internal Evidence Tags or External Evidence Tags and tape it to the front of your clothing.
2. Form circles of at least six students. There are six categories of evidence (three internal evidence categories and three external evidence categories), so be sure that at least one evidence tag from each category is represented in the circle of students.
3. Select a soft, lightweight ball or object that can be safely tossed from person to person. You will categorize the tags on other students to identify whether their tags belong to the internal evidence group or external evidence group.
4. Toss the ball to someone wearing a label that corresponds with the term your teacher calls out, either "external evidence!" or "internal evidence!" If you toss the ball to someone wearing evidence in the wrong category (e.g. tossing the ball to someone labeled with an archeological discovery when "internal evidence" was called), then you must sit down. You may still participate in the game but must remain seated. The last student standing wins the round.
5. If time permits, your teacher may change the groups so you can interact with a different set of evidence.

CH 3

Chapter 3 Review

Take notes during the slide presentation.

Chapter 3 Study Guide

Key Terms
church fathers
Dead Sea Scrolls
textual variants
lost gospels
gnosticism

Key Verses
Proverbs 30:5–6
2 Peter 3:15–16
1 John 1:1
2 Peter 1:20–21

1. What is authority, and what does it mean to submit to God's authority?

2. Use internal evidence to defend the Old Testament's authority.

3. Give specific examples of how Jesus confirmed his trust in the Old Testament.

4. Describe the internal evidence for the apostles' intent and authority for writing the New Testament.

5. Identify specific examples of external evidence that support the Old Testament's reliability.

6. List the ancient non-biblical writings that confirm the historicity of Jesus and the teaching of the early Christians.

7. Describe the role of eyewitness testimony and the church fathers in affirming the accuracy of the Gospels.

CH 3 Study Guide *(continued)*

8. Explain how the Dead Sea Scrolls and many available early New Testament manuscripts confirm the accurate preservation of the biblical writings.

9. Briefly appraise and formulate responses to the three common objections to the reliability and authority of the Bible.

10. Summarize five areas of life that are under God's authority, and classify daily activities into those five categories.

11. Describe the importance of examining and evaluating all truth claims..

12. Explain why God wants people to obey him.

13. What are the Dead Sea Scrolls, and what is their importance?

14. What are textual variants? Explain their significance to the Bible.

15. Are the lost gospels part of the Bible? If not, explain what they are.

16. What is gnosticism?

17. Explain the difference between internal evidence and external evidence in relation to the reliability of the Bible.

18. What is radical individualism, and how does it compare with the Christian relationship to authority?

19. Who affirmed the authority of the apostle Paul's writings?

20. Explain why some people resist God's authority.

21. Read and study the four Key Verses listed at the top of the study guide.

4

How to Read the Bible

How to Read the Bible

Chapter 4 Syllabus

Lesson		Assignment		Page
1	In Class	REVIEW	Chapter 3 Test	
	In Class	DISCUSS	Questions for Chapter 4.1–4.2	66–67
	In Class	EXPLORE	Activity: According to God's Word	67
	At Home	READ	Chapter 4.3–4.4	ST 51–53
	At Home	ANSWER	Questions for Chapter 4.3–4.4	68–69
2	In Class	DISCUSS	Questions for Chapter 4.3–4.4	
	In Class	EXPLORE	Activity: Self-Centered or God-Centered?	69
	At Home	READ	Chapter 4.5–4.6	ST 53–56
	At Home	ANSWER	Questions for Chapter 4.5–4.6	70–71
3	In Class	DISCUSS	Questions for Chapter 4.5–4.6	
	In Class	EXPLORE	Activity: Common Mistakes in Bible Reading	71
	At Home	READ	Chapter 4.7–4.8	ST 56–59
	At Home	ANSWER	Questions for Chapter 4.7–4.8	72–73
4	In Class	DISCUSS	Questions for Chapter 4.7–4.8	
	In Class	EXPLORE	Activity: Steps to Reading the Bible Well	73
	At Home	READ	Chapter 4.9–4.10	ST 59–61
	At Home	ANSWER	Questions for Chapter 4.9–4.10	74–75
5	In Class	DISCUSS	Questions for Chapter 4.9–4.10	
	In Class	EXPLORE	Activity: Historic Journals	75
6	In Class	EXPLORE	Activity: Bible Reading and Study	
7	In Class	WATCH	Videos	
	In Class	ANSWER	Video Questions	76–78
	In Class	DISCUSS	Video Questions	
8	In Class	EXPLORE	Activity: Ad to Promote Bible Reading	79
	In Class	REVIEW FOR	Chapter 4 Test	80
9	In Class	STUDY FOR	Chapter 4 Test	
	In Class	ANSWER	Study Guide Questions	81–83
10	In Class	TAKE	Chapter 4 Test	
	At Home	READ	Chapter 5.1–5.2	ST 62–65
	At Home	ANSWER	Questions for Chapter 5.1–5.2	86

*Student Textbook (ST) Student Manual (SM)

CH 4

Chapter 4.1–4.2

DISCUSSION QUESTIONS

1. What problems do you see with how the students are reading the Bible in the illustration? [4.1]

2. How have you seen similar problems in Bible studies with your peers? If you were to lead a Bible study, what might you do to minimize or address such problems? [4.1]

3. What makes the Bible difficult to understand and apply? [4.1]

4. What impact did the invention of the printing press have on Bible reading? [4.2]

5. Were you surprised by the statistics on Bible reading? Why or why not? How do you think a Bible reading plan might affect the way people think and make choices in their lives? Have you ever used a Bible reading plan? If so, what was it like? [4.2]

6. Why was the statement "Pick it up and read it" so powerful for Augustine? [4.2]

Activity

ACCORDING TO GOD'S WORD

OBJECTIVE:

You will identify the benefits of Bible reading according to Psalm 119.

PREPARATION:

- Materials needed: Bible, paper, and pen
- Time required: 10–15 minutes

PROCEDURE:

1. Turn to Psalm 119. This psalm is divided into 22 sections, and each section corresponds with a letter of the Hebrew alphabet. Your teacher will assign you a section of the psalm. If another student has the same section, you may work together.
2. Read your section and identify any benefits it suggests come from studying God's Word. You have five minutes for this task.
3. Be ready to share the answers you found.

CH 4

Chapter 4.3–4.4

DISCUSSION QUESTIONS

1. Explain why people never "arrive" in their study of Scripture. [4.3]

2. How is considering the study of Scripture as a lifelong journey good news? [4.3]

3. Is it wrong to ask, "What does this mean to me?" when it comes to the Bible? Why or why not? [4.4]

4. What is postmodernism, and how does it relate to the study of the Bible? [4.4]

5. What are the dangers of reading the Bible with a postmodern or self-centered approach? [4.4]

Activity

SELF-CENTERED OR GOD-CENTERED?

OBJECTIVE:

You will tell a Bible story from a self-centered focus and then from a God-centered focus.

PREPARATION:

- Materials needed: Bible
- Time required: 15–20 minutes

PROCEDURE:

1. Note that many Sunday school stories are presented with a self-centered focus rather than a God-centered focus. For example, the story of Daniel in the lions' den (Daniel 6:1–28) could be looked at with a self-centered focus (Daniel did what was right, so God took care of him). The story could also be seen with a God-centered focus (per Daniel 6:25–27, a decree was sent out so that all people would learn about God).
2. Your teacher will assign your group one of the following passages:
   - Group 1: David defeats Goliath (1 Samuel 17:1–58)
   - Group 2: Solomon prays for wisdom (1 Kings 3:1–15 and 10:23–24)
   - Group 3: The fiery furnace (Daniel 3:1–30)
3. Discuss the story with your group, referring to the Bible passages as needed. Half of your group will tell the story from a self-centered view, and the other half will tell it from a God-centered view. Present your perspectives to the class.

CH 4

Chapter 4.5–4.6

DISCUSSION QUESTIONS

1. Why does the Bible need to be interpreted? Why can't we just read it? [4.5]

2. Why is it a mistake to assume that the Bible applies uniquely to us? [4.5]

3. What are the potential dangers of reading the Bible through the lens of a systematic theology? [4.5]

4. What is context, and why is it important for understanding the Bible? [4.6]

5. What does it mean to say the Bible is eternally relevant and historically particular? [4.6]

Activity

COMMON MISTAKES IN BIBLE READING

OBJECTIVE:

You will analyze Scripture in view of five common mistakes made in Bible reading.

PREPARATION:

- Materials needed: TR 4.3A and Bible
- Time required: 15–20 minutes

PROCEDURE:

1. Read TR 4.3A Common Mistakes in Bible Reading.
2. With a partner, discuss and answer the questions. Bibles will be needed for some exercises.
3. As a class, take turns sharing answers.

CH 4

Chapter 4.7–4.8

DISCUSSION QUESTIONS

1. What is exegesis? [4.7]

2. What are three different types of Bible translations, and how do they differ from one another? [4.7]

3. What is the difference between historical context and literary context? [4.7–4.8]

4. Why is it so important to understand the genre of a biblical book? Illustrate your answer by giving two examples using Bible verses in different genres. [4.8]

5. What three things should a good commentary supply? [4.8]

6. What is the difference between a descriptive and a prescriptive passage? What are some examples of each? [4.8]

Activity

STEPS TO READING THE BIBLE WELL

OBJECTIVE:
You will present steps to reading the Bible well.

PREPARATION:
- Materials needed: student textbook
- Time required: 20–25 minutes

PROCEDURE:
1. Your group will be assigned one of the seven steps to reading the Bible well from Chapter 4.7—4.8. Create a two-minute skit to illustrate the step in reading the Bible well that your group was assigned.
2. Assign roles to each group member and practice the skit.
3. Present your skit to the class.

CH 4

Chapter 4.9–4.10

DISCUSSION QUESTIONS

1. How does the Holy Spirit help us as we read Scripture? [4.9]

2. What does it mean to be "doers of the word" (James 1:22)? [4.9]

3. What are three ways to become a doer of the word? [4.9]

4. Do believers experience doubt? Explain. [4.10]

5. What should Christians do with their doubts? [4.10]

Activity

HISTORIC JOURNALS

OBJECTIVE:

You will compare autobiographical excerpts to assess the value of writing what you are learning from Scripture and in your walk with Christ.

PREPARATION:

- Materials needed: TR 4.5A and pencil
- Time required: 10–15 minutes

PROCEDURE:

1. Read TR 4.5A Historic Journals.
2. Identify at least four benefits of keeping a record of one's spiritual life.
3. Take turns discussing your findings with the class.

CH 4

Videos

DISCUSSION QUESTIONS

Read the discussion questions before each video is played so that you know what to listen for.

Video 1: How Can We Communicate Truth in Our Culture?

1. What example shows we live in a culture where truth has become relative?

2. How do we know that truth matters to people?

3. What strategy can be used to converse with people who are relativists?

4. How does the content of this video relate to the Bible study gone wrong in Chapter 4.1?

Video 2: Why Should We Consider the Bible an Authority?

1. How is the Bible different from other books, such as those written by Shakespeare or Aristotle?

2. What arguments are given for believing the Bible is true?

3. How did Jesus treat Scripture?

Video 3: What Causes the Bible to Often Be Misunderstood?

1. Why is it so easy for people to misunderstand the Bible?

2. What is the first step of the two-step process the speaker shared to help readers understand the Bible?

3. What is the second step of the process?

▶ Video 4: How Can the Church Encourage Healthy Biblical Engagement?

1. What is a Scripture McNugget®?

2. Should Christians live on a diet of Scripture McNuggets®? Why or why not?

3. What are some common Scripture McNuggets® you see today?

▶ Video 5: Developing Healthy Habits around Personal Bible Study

1. What is the difference between Bible reading and Bible study?

2. What books of the Bible have you read in their entirety?

CH 4

Videos (continued)

Video 6: Students Share Why the Bible Is Important

1. What reasons do students give for considering the Bible important?

2. What additional reasons could you give for considering the Bible important?

3. A student in the video shares her favorite Bible verse. Which verse is it?

Video 7: Facing Our Doubts as Christians

1. Reading and study of the Bible can sometimes cause people to experience doubt. The speaker describes three causes of doubt. What are they?

2. How should you deal with each kind of doubt?

Activity

AD TO PROMOTE BIBLE READING

OBJECTIVE

You will design a full-page advertisement or make a thirty-second commercial encouraging people to read Scripture.

PREPARATION:

- Materials needed: Bible, markers, and large paper
- Time required: 20–30 minutes

PROCEDURE:

1. Your teacher will divide the class into five groups.
2. Your group will be assigned Bible verses from one of the following sets:
   Group 1: Psalm 1:1–2, Ezra 7:10, Romans 15:4
   Group 2: John 20:30–31, Acts 8:35, Colossians 3:16
   Group 3: Joshua 1:8, 2 Peter 3:1–2, Acts 17:11
   Group 4: Proverbs 30:5, Revelation 1:3, Luke 4:16
   Group 5: Psalm 37:31, Psalm 40:8, Matthew 7:24
3. With your group, determine how your verses encourage people to read the Bible today. Then, brainstorm how to express this encouragement to teenagers.
4. Decide whether to make a print advertisement or demonstrate a commercial. Obtain markers and large paper if you design a print advertisement.
5. Present the ad or commercial to the class.

CH 4

Chapter 4 Review

Take notes during the slide presentation.

Chapter 4 Study Guide

Key Terms
postmodernism
hermeneutics
context
exegesis
historical context
literary context

Key Verses
2 Timothy 2:15
2 Timothy 3:16–17
James 1:22
1 Thessalonians 2:13

1. How should you *not* do a Bible study?

2. Why is personal Bible reading necessary?

3. What are the different benefits of studying God's Word?

4. In what ways has postmodernism affected the study of the Bible?

5. What are five common mistakes people make when reading the Bible?

CH 4 Study Guide *(continued)*

6. Explain the seven steps to reading the Bible well.

7. What are three ways to apply what you learn in Bible study?

8. Why do most people find the Bible hard to understand?

9. What are three kinds of translations? What does each type of translation seek to do?

10. How do commentaries help people understand the content and context of Scripture?

11. What is the difference between a descriptive and a prescriptive passage of Scripture?

12. What role does the Holy Spirit have in our reading of Scripture?

13. What should you do if you experience doubt when reading Scripture?

14. Read and study the four Key Verses listed at the top of the study guide.

5

The Bible as a Story

The Bible as a Story

Chapter 5 Syllabus

Lesson		Assignment		Page
1	In Class	REVIEW	Chapter 4 Test	
	In Class	DISCUSS	Questions for Chapter 5.1–5.2	86
	In Class	EXPLORE	Activity: Anatomy of a Bible Story	87-88
	At Home	READ	Chapter 5.3–5.4	ST 65–67
	At Home	ANSWER	Questions for Chapter 5.3–5.4	89–90
2	In Class	DISCUSS	Questions for Chapter 5.3–5.4	
	In Class	EXPLORE	Activity: Worldview Bingo	90
	At Home	READ	Chapter 5.5–5.6	ST 68–70
	At Home	ANSWER	Questions for Chapter 5.5–5.6	91–92
3	In Class	DISCUSS	Questions for Chapter 5.5–5.6	
	In Class	EXPLORE	Activity: Literary Attributes	92
	At Home	READ	Chapter 5.7–5.8	ST 70–72
	At Home	ANSWER	Questions for Chapter 5.7–5.8	93–94
4	In Class	DISCUSS	Questions for Chapter 5.7–5.8	
	In Class	EXPLORE	Activity: Stories within a Story	94
	At Home	READ	Chapter 5.9–5.10	ST 72–75
	At Home	ANSWER	Questions for Chapter 5.9–5.10	95–96
5	In Class	DISCUSS	Questions for Chapter 5.9–5.10	
	In Class	EXPLORE	Activity: God's Story Bible Study	96
6	In Class	EXPLORE	Activity: Building a Metanarrative	
7	In Class	WATCH	Videos	
	In Class	ANSWER	Video Questions	97–99
	In Class	DISCUSS	Video Questions	
8	In Class	EXPLORE	Activity: Narrative Quiz Game	100
	In Class	REVIEW FOR	Chapter 5 Test	101
9	In Class	STUDY FOR	Chapter 5 Test	
	In Class	ANSWER	Study Guide Questions	102–105
10	In Class	TAKE	Chapter 5 Test	
	At Home	READ	Chapter 6.1–6.2	ST 76–79
	At Home	ANSWER	Questions for Chapter 6.1–6.2	108–109

*Student Textbook (ST) Student Manual (SM)

CH 5 Chapter 5.1–5.2

DISCUSSION QUESTIONS

1. In what ways do stories shape the way we live? [5.1]

2. What are the main elements of good stories? Explain why these elements are important. [5.2]

3. What are the three parts of the three-act story structure? Explain why this structure is helpful. [5.2]

4. How is each of our lives like a story? [5.2]

Activity

ANATOMY OF A BIBLE STORY

OBJECTIVE:

You will analyze a Bible story for the components of good storytelling.

PREPARATION:

- Materials needed: Bible, paper, and pen
- Time required: 20–25 minutes

PROCEDURE:

1. Work with a partner to choose a favorite bible story from the list below. Indicate your choice with a checkmark.
    - The Tower of Babel (Genesis 11:1–9)
    - The Birth of Moses (Exodus 1:22, 2:1–10)
    - Moses Strikes the Rock (Numbers 20:1–13)
    - Jesus Teaches His Disciples about the Sabbath (Matthew 12:1–14)
    - Jesus Appears to His Disciples (John 20:11–23)
    - The Healing of Aeneas and Dorcas (Acts 9: 32–43)
2. Work with your partner to identify the components of a well-written story and answer the questions in the Anatomy of a Bible Story Study on the next page.
3. Write down your findings, and as time allows, present them to the class.

Activity

ANATOMY OF A BIBLE STORY STUDY

1. Describe the following elements you identified in your Bible story:
   - Setting:
   - Characters:
   - Conflict:
   - Theme:
   - Plot:
   - Point of View:

2. How do style and tone contribute to a story?

Chapter 5.3–5.4

DISCUSSION QUESTIONS

1. What is a metanarrative? Give some examples of metanarratives. [5.3]

2. How can metanarratives help us understand the meaning of our lives and make sense of the world around us? [5.3–5.4]

3. What is the relationship between a metanarrative and a worldview? [5.4]

4. Name some worldviews that are popular today. Do you think the metanarratives they teach can provide meaningful answers to life's biggest questions? [5.4]

5.3–5.4 *(continued)*

5. Are all worldviews equally valid? If so, why? If not, how can we know which worldview is best? [5.4]

Activity

WORLDVIEW BINGO

OBJECTIVE:

You will identify the elements of six common worldviews.

PREPARATION:

- Materials needed: TR 5.2A and pen
- Time required: 20–25 minutes

PROCEDURE:

1. Your teacher will give you one card from TR 5.2A Worldview Bingo. As your teacher calls out a worldview, mark all boxes that apply with the appropriate symbol. The symbols are as follows:
   - secularism = stick figure
   - new spirituality = three interlocking circles
   - postmodernism = arrow
   - Marxism = star
   - Islam = half-moon
   - Christianity = cross

(Note: Some bingo boxes may apply to more than one worldview, but you should only mark each box once.)

2. The goal is to complete at least one row correctly or complete the highest number of correct rows. When you have completed your first row, you should raise your hand and call out "bingo." Take your sheet to your teacher to check the answers. If your row is correct, the teacher will record that you had the first complete row. If the row is incorrect, then you are out. If you are unsure that your first completed row is correct, you may choose to wait until completing a second row before saying "bingo."

Chapter 5.5–5.6

DISCUSSION QUESTIONS

1. What kind of story does the Bible tell? [5.5]

2. What genres are present in the Bible, and how do they relate to the historical narrative? [5.5]

3. What significance does the historical narrative of the Bible have for our lives? [5.5]

4. What does it mean to say that the Bible is comprehensive? [5.6]

CH 5

5.5–5.6 *(continued)*

5. What does it mean to say that the Bible is coherent? [5.6]

6. What does it mean to say that the Bible is normative? [5.6]

Activity

LITERARY ATTRIBUTES

OBJECTIVE:

You will create a memory aid to help you remember the three literary attributes of the Bible.

PREPARATION:

- Materials needed: poster board and markers
- Time required: 20–25 minutes

PROCEDURE:

1. For this activity, you will work together in groups of three or four students. Recall the background information about the Bible: that in addition to being a historical narrative, the Bible has three literary attributes: it is comprehensive, coherent, and normative.
2. Using the poster board and markers, work with your group to brainstorm and design symbols, acronyms, rhymes, or visual cues to help you recall the three literary attributes described in the lesson.
3. Present your memory aids to the class.

Chapter 5.7–5.8

DISCUSSION QUESTIONS

1. What does it mean to be caught up in God's big story? [5.7]

2. How aware were the biblical authors of their part in God's story? [5.7]

3. Who are some of the biblical characters who found themselves caught up in God's big story? [5.7]

4. Listed below are three ways people summarize the message of the Bible. Explain why each is faulty. [5.8]

- Creation, Fall, Redemption
- We are sinners, Jesus died for our sins, those who trust Jesus go to heaven when they die.
- The God of the Old Testament was cruel, but Jesus is kind. He sets a good example that we are to follow.

CH 5

5.7–5.8 *(continued)*

5. In your own words, explain what happens in each of the six acts of the biblical outline. Use the chart in Chapter 5.8 of your textbook as a reference. Which act do you feel you understand the best? The least? [5.8]

6. Is the biblical metanarrative about individuals or the world? Explain. [5.8]

Activity

STORIES WITHIN A STORY

OBJECTIVE:
You will create a visual representation of the biblical metanarrative and where well-known Bible stories fit within it.

PREPARATION:
- Materials needed: Bible, paper, and pen or marker
- Time required: 20–25 minutes

PROCEDURE:

1. On a piece of paper, draw a horizontal line and mark it with small vertical lines to show the main parts of the biblical metanarrative.
2. Place the following well-known Bible narratives on the line within the proper section of the metanarrative timeline.
   - Joseph is sold into slavery.
   - Adam and Eve are thrown out of the garden.
   - Jesus heals a blind man.
   - David defeats Goliath.
   - Jonah goes on a mission to Nineveh.
   - Paul and Silas are thrown in jail.
   - Esther saves the Jewish people.
   - The Israelites receive the Law at Mount Sinai.
   - Jesus returns on a white horse.
3. Present your work to the class.

Chapter 5.9–5.10

DISCUSSION QUESTIONS

1. How does the Author of the Bible's great story get involved in the story? [5.9]

2. What can we do when we find troubling or difficult things in the Bible? [5.9]

3. What do you think C. S. Lewis meant when he said that Jesus' love for us is "quite relentless in its determination that we shall be cured of [our] sins, at whatever cost to us, at whatever cost to Him"? Is this good news or bad news? [5.9]

4. What can we learn about God's nature and character from reading the Bible as one grand story? [5.9]

CH 5

5.9–5.10 *(continued)*

5. Based on what you have read in this chapter, what part do you think Christians have to play in God's great story? [5.10]

Activity

GOD'S STORY BIBLE STUDY

OBJECTIVE:

You will apply what you have learned about the biblical metanarrative to the story of Jonah.

PREPARATION:

- Materials needed: TR 5.5A, Bible, and pen
- Time required: 20–30 minutes

PROCEDURE:

1. Read the instructions on TR 5.5A God's Story Bible Study. Then, review the story of Jonah in your Bible. Use the steps from the instruction sheet to complete Exercise: Jonah and God's Grand Story.
2. Be prepared to share your thoughts with the class.

Videos

DISCUSSION QUESTIONS

Read the discussion questions before each video is played so that you know what to listen for.

Video 1: How Do We Fit into God's Story?

1. What claim does Genesis 1:1 make about the Bible's message?

2. What kind of truth does the Bible offer?

3. What are the two main purposes people were created for?

4. How do modern Christians fit into God's story?

Video 2: How Can We Effectively Understand the Scripture?

1. What is one of the first steps Christians can take to understand the Bible?

2. What does it mean to receive the Bible?

Video 3: What Is the Difference Between Mormonism and Christianity?

1. What are the two primary differences between Mormonism and Christianity?

CH 5

Videos *(continued)*

2. How are the Mormon and Christian views of God different?

3. How are the Mormon and Christian views of salvation different?

Video 4: How Should Christians Handle Apparent Biblical Contradictions?

1. What is the key for interpreting difficult Bible passages properly?

2. What is the art and science of biblical interpretation?

3. Should we base important doctrines on verses we don't understand well?

4. What is biblical interpretation based on?

5. What kind of systematic approach should we take to interpreting Scripture?

Video 5: What Is the Christian Metanarrative?

1. What are the three questions the Christian metanarrative answers?

2. According to the speaker, what are the four acts of the metanarrative?

3. What four words describe the metanarrative?

Video 6: Where Do I Fit in Christianity?

1. How does the speaker briefly describe the Christian story?

2. What does the metanarrative mean for us personally?

3. Why should the fact that God knows our hearts comfort us?

Activity

NARRATIVE QUIZ GAME

OBJECTIVE

You will review key terms and concepts from the lesson.

PREPARATION:

- Materials needed: none
- Time required: 20–30 minutes

PROCEDURE:

1. Your teacher will divide the class into three or four teams. Work with your group to play the game.
2. Follow along as your teacher reads the game rules.
   a. Teams will choose a category and a clue by saying, for example, "Metanarrative for 600." Teams must choose clues in the same column until that column has been completed. (For example, if Team A choses the Metanarrative 200 clue, Team B must choose a clue from the Metanarrative category. All teams will choose from the same category until that column has been completed.)
   b. After the clue has been chosen, read the slide for that clue aloud. Teams have 15 seconds to quietly confer. When a team is ready to answer the clue, one student from the team will stand. The team member who stood up the fastest will be called on to play. Students have ten seconds to answer the clue.
   c. Answers are given in a "who" or "what" question form. For example, "What is a story?" or "Who is Jesus?" If the fastest team answers correctly, the points for that clue will be added to the team's score. If the team answers incorrectly, the same number of points will be lost. Then, the second-fastest team may take a guess. If correct, that team receives the points. If they are incorrect, the third-fastest team can make a guess. The team that answers correctly chooses the next clue. If no one answers correctly, the team that chose the previous clue chooses again.
3. As teams correctly answer clues, your teacher will record their points. At the end of the game, your teacher will tally up the points and announce the winner. The team with the most points at the end of the game wins.

Chapter 5 Review

Take notes during the slide presentation.

CH 5

Chapter 5 Study Guide

Key Terms

narrative
metanarrative
historical narrative
comprehensive
coherent
normative

Key Verses

Mark 1:14–15
Romans 1:1–5
Galatians 4:4
Revelation 21:5

1. Explain why stories are important.

2. List the different components of well-formed narratives.

3. Explain the relationship between metanarratives, worldviews, and the meaning of life.

4. Identify and critique the postmodern view of metanarratives.

5. Compare and contrast common non-Christian worldviews.

6. Summarize the metanarrative of the Bible.

7. What is a historical narrative? Defend the Bible as a historical narrative.

8. Identify biblical characters who were aware they were part of God's larger story.

9. Describe the six main acts in the biblical metanarrative and relate them to their corresponding Scripture.

10. Explain God's role in the biblical metanarrative.

CH 5 Study Guide *(continued)*

11. Explain the importance of knowing that the Bible is a metanarrative when interpreting difficult passages.

12. What is a narrative? What is a metanarrative?

13. What are some examples of fiction or nonfiction metanarratives?

14. What does it mean to say that the Bible is comprehensive?

15. What does it mean to say that the Bible is coherent?

16. Describe the typical three-act structure of most story plots.

17. List the big questions that worldviews and their metanarratives seek to answer.

18. What type of worldview do we need? What worldview best serves this purpose?

19. What is the climax of the biblical metanarrative?

20. What does the Bible's internal coherence indicate?

21. Read and study the four Key Verses listed at the beginning of the study guide.

6

Act 1: Creation

Chapter 6 Syllabus

Lesson		Assignment		Page
1	In Class	REVIEW	Chapter 5 Test	
	In Class	DISCUSS	Questions for Chapter 6.1–6.2	108–109
	In Class	EXPLORE	Activity: Creating a Creation Myth	109
	At Home	READ	Chapter 6.3–6.4	ST 79–81
	At Home	ANSWER	Questions for Chapter 6.3–6.4	110–111
2	In Class	DISCUSS	Questions for Chapter 6.3–6.4	
	In Class	EXPLORE	Activity: Praising the Creator	111
	At Home	READ	Chapter 6.5–6.6	ST 81–84
	At Home	ANSWER	Questions for Chapter 6.5–6.6	112–113
3	In Class	DISCUSS	Questions for Chapter 6.5–6.6	
	In Class	EXPLORE	Activity: Community Stewardship Plan	113–114
	At Home	READ	Chapter 6.7–6.8	ST 84–87
	At Home	ANSWER	Questions for Chapter 6.7–6.8	115
4	In Class	DISCUSS	Questions for Chapter 6.7–6.8	
	In Class	EXPLORE	Activity: Reasons to Believe in God	116
	At Home	READ	Chapter 6.9–6.10	ST 87–90
	At Home	ANSWER	Questions for Chapter 6.9–6.10	117
5	In Class	DISCUSS	Questions for Chapter 6.9–6.10	
	In Class	EXPLORE	Activity: Gender and Marriage	118
6	In Class	EXPLORE	Activity: Creation Feud Game	
7	In Class	WATCH	Videos	
	In Class	ANSWER	Video Questions	119–120
	In Class	DISCUSS	Video Questions	
8	In Class	EXPLORE	Activity: Who Is God and Who Are Humans?	121
	In Class	REVIEW FOR	Chapter 6 Test	122
9	In Class	STUDY FOR	Chapter 6 Test	
	In Class	ANSWER	Study Guide Questions	123–125
10	In Class	TAKE	Chapter 6 Test	
	At Home	READ	Chapter 7.1–7.2	ST 91–94
	At Home	ANSWER	Questions for Chapter 7.1–7.2	128

*Student Textbook (ST) Student Manual (SM)

CH 6 Chapter 6.1–6.2

DISCUSSION QUESTIONS

1. What is a creation myth? What are some examples of creation myths? [6.1]

2. What similarities are there between the Genesis creation account and the *Enuma Elish?* Do you notice any differences? [6.1]

3. In what ways do we see evidence of the Trinity in Genesis 1? [6.2]

4. What is significant about being made in God's image? [6.2]

5. The creation account in Genesis 1 is shockingly brief. It leaves many things out and many questions unanswered. Why do you think this is so? What might this tell you about what kind of story Genesis 1 is trying to tell? [6.2]

Activity

CREATING A CREATION MYTH

OBJECTIVE:

You will write an original myth that expresses an idea of how people may have explained creation without the Bible.

PREPARATION:

- Materials needed: paper and pen
- Time required: 20–25 minutes

PROCEDURE:

1. Listen as your teacher reads two creation myths. Share your observations about any significant details.
2. Write your own creation myth using the guidelines below. You will have 12 minutes.
2. The following information must be included in the myth: who or what did the creating, what was created, how it was created, and what the differences and similarities are between the creator and the creation.
3. Compare your myth with the eight significant details of the biblical creation account.
4. Share your creation myth with the class, and discuss how the myths differ from the biblical creation story.

CH 6

Chapter 6.3–6.4

DISCUSSION QUESTIONS

1. What does it mean that God rested on the seventh day? [6.3]

2. Why is work a good thing? What kinds of work have you found especially meaningful or fulfilling? [6.3]

3. **What is significant about the creation of the woman in Genesis 2? [6.3]**

4. What implications do you think this has for the way women are treated in society today? [6.3]

5. How does the universe reflect the glory of God? What aspect of God's amazing world do you enjoy the most? [6.4]

6. Why did God create humans and the world? [6.4]

7. What does it mean to say that God is transcendent and immanent? [6.4]

Activity

PRAISING THE CREATOR

OBJECTIVE:

You will find a New Testament verse about creation and explain why the Bible refers to creation throughout Scripture.

PREPARATION:

- Materials needed: Bible, concordance or computer, paper, and pen
- Time required: 20–25 minutes

PROCEDURE:

1. Each person in your group will find and write down one New Testament passage that refers to creation in some way. You may use a Bible, concordance, or computer to help with your research.
2. Take turns reading your verses to the rest of your group.
3. Discuss with the class why the Bible refers to creation throughout the Scriptures and not just in the book of Genesis.
4. If time allows, use the words from your group's verses to write a psalm of praise to God. If you would like, you may write your psalm to a tune from a familiar song.
5. Share your psalm with the rest of the class.

CH 6

Chapter 6.5–6.6

DISCUSSION QUESTIONS

1. Describe three common views of what it means to be made in God's image. [6.5]

2. How are the ideas of image-bearing and stewardship connected? [6.5]

3. What does it mean to be a sub-creator? What are some examples of sub-creation? [6.5]

4. How does the Bible describe our relationship with God? Which description do you find most comforting? Which is most challenging to you? [6.6]

5. What is the purpose of our sexuality? [6.6]

6. What is a marriage according to Genesis 1–2? [6.6]

Activity

COMMUNITY STEWARDSHIP PLAN

OBJECTIVE:

You will devise a stewardship plan for a specific need in your community.

PREPARATION:

- Materials needed: pen
- Time required: 20–25 minutes

PROCEDURE:

1. With your group, choose a geographical area or environmental issue in your community that needs care.
2. Work together to make a community stewardship plan. Fill out the plan on the next page.
3. Be ready to share your plan with the class.

Activity

COMMUNITY STEWARDSHIP PLAN

Group members' names:

Geographical area or environmental issue in your community that needs stewardship:

What is your action plan to provide stewardship for this area or issue?

Who will need to help you with this project?

What equipment or supplies will you need?

How can you let people know about your stewardship plan to get them involved?

Chapter 6.7–6.8

DISCUSSION QUESTIONS

1. Does Genesis promote the exploitation of the natural world? Why or why not? [6.7]

2. What are some practical ways that we can steward the natural world? [6.7]

3. How does Genesis 1–2 confront ancient pagan creation myths? What makes Genesis 1–2 different from these myths? [6.8]

4. Compared to Egyptian culture as described in the Old Testament, how does Genesis 1–2 uphold human dignity? [6.8]

CH 6

6.7–6.8 *(continued)*

Activity

REASONS TO BELIEVE IN GOD

OBJECTIVE:

You will compile a list of 10 reasons to believe in God.

PREPARATION:

- Materials needed: student textbook, computer, paper, and pen
- Time required: 20–30 minutes

PROCEDURE:

1. Your teacher will have you work independently or with a partner.
2. Make a list of 10 reasons to believe in God. These reasons should be based on forensic and historic evidence.
3. You may use the information from Chapters 1–6 in your textbooks and any significant evidence you may have found researching on the internet.
4. Share your reasons with the class. As the class shares their reasons, someone will write them on the board. If the same reason is given more than once, a mark will be placed next to the reason each time it is mentioned.
5. Were there any reasons that were mentioned only once? Discuss which types of evidence were mentioned the most.
6. The purpose of this list is to help you know how to defend your faith and belief in the existence of God. If time allows, write a paragraph or two to someone who is skeptical about the existence of God. Include your 10 reasons in your paragraph. Memorize either your paragraph or your 10 reasons so you are prepared to give an answer (1 Peter 3:15) to an unbeliever.

Chapter 6.9–6.10

DISCUSSION QUESTIONS

1. How does Genesis 1–2 confront alternative worldviews? What are some examples? [6.9]

2. How might seeing people as made in God's image make a difference in racism, sexism, abortion, and euthanasia? [6.9]

3. How does Christianity uphold the goodness of the body and sexuality compared with secular views of sexuality? [6.9]

6.9–6.10 (continued)

Activity

GENDER AND MARRIAGE

OBJECTIVE:
You will explain why there are only two genders and be able to defend marriage.

PREPARATION:
- Materials needed: paper and pen
- Time required: 25–30 minutes

PROCEDURE:
1. You are going to watch two videos—one about gender and the other about marriage. Take notes during the videos. After watching them, be prepared to participate in class discussion.

- Video 1: *Why Did God Only Create Two Genders*?
- Video 2: *How To: Defend Marriage*

Videos

DISCUSSION QUESTIONS

Read the discussion questions before each video is played so you know what to listen for.

Video 1: Is the Belief in Creation Important?

1. Why is the topic of creation important to the Christian worldview?

2. The speaker said that we need to begin at the beginning. Why do you think she said that?

3. Science answers how things came into being. Religion answers things such as moral questions and the meaning of human life. Do you think these two domains can be separated? Why or why not?

Video 2: What Makes the Christian Worldview the "Right" One?

1. Why does the speaker believe the Christian worldview is accurate?

2. What example of a particular does the speaker give?

3. Does that example of a particular fit the Christian worldview? How?

4. Does the idea of evil being in the world fit with atheism? Why or why not?

Video 3: Why Is Biblical Marriage So Important?

1. Regarding the topic of marriage, what ultimately matters?

2. What does God say marriage is?

3. What are the benefits of operating in God's design for marriage?

CH 6 Videos *(continued)*

4. Is God trying to limit our freedom or restrict our options concerning marriage? Explain.

Video 4: Why Does It Matter When I Have Sex?

1. Why is sex important to God?

2. God could have created a suitable helper for Adam in many ways. Why did he make Eve Adam's suitable helper?

3. What do you think the world would be like if God created human beings to reproduce by just getting wet?

4. What is it that you are doing if you sin sexually?

5. Why do you think it is so significant to sin against your own body?

Video 5: If Pornography Only Hurts Me, Is It Really that Bad?

1. In what four ways is pornography harmful?

2. Most abuse is directed at women. What is wrong with this type of abuse?

3. What happens when individuals have massive amounts of exposure to pornography?

4. How did listening to the information in this video make you feel? How do you think God feels about his children being abused? What are some things you can do to stop pornography and sex trafficking?

Activity

WHO IS GOD AND WHO ARE HUMANS?

OBJECTIVE:

You will identify and analyze the attributes of God and the characteristics of humans.

PREPARATION:

- Materials needed: Bible, student textbcok, 10 index cards per group, and pen
- Time required: 20–30 minutes

PROCEDURE:

1. Your teacher will divide the class into groups and give each group 10 index cards.
2. Remember that an attribute of God is an inherent quality or feature of the character of God. An attribute of God will answer the question: Who is God? A characteristic of humans describes the nature and features of people, and answers the question: Who are humans?
3. Your group will be assigned to identify either the attributes of God or the characteristics of humans. You may use your textbook and Genesis 1–2 in your Bible.
4. Work with your group to fill out the index cards. Write one attribute of God or one characteristic of humans at the top of each card. Then write a description of the evidence for that attribute or characteristic on the same card.

   Example:

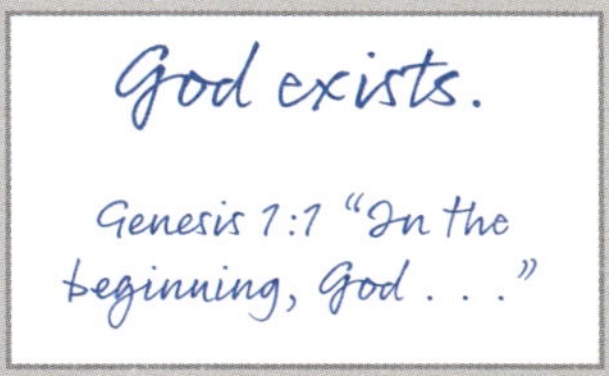

5. You will have 10–12 minutes to complete all your cards.
6. Share the items your group wrote with the class. Your teacher will write them in the appropriate columns on the chart. As attributes or characteristics are repeated, your teacher will place a check mark by the repeated feature.
7. When finished, discuss the collection of God's attributes. Which attributes of God were most observed? Which attribute is most surprising or unusual? Are there any attributes of God missing from this list? Which attributes would you use to tell someone about who God is? Repeat the first three questions for the characteristics of humans and then compare them to the attributes of God.

CH 6

Chapter 6 Review

Take notes during the slide presentation.

Chapter 6 Study Guide

Key Terms

creation myth
Elohim
imago Dei
Yahweh
transcendence
immanence
stewardship

Key Verses

Genesis 1:1
Genesis 1:26–28
Genesis 1:31
Genesis 2:18
Psalm 8:4–6

1. What is a creation myth? Explain the purpose of creation myths.

2. Summarize the creation narrative from Genesis 1.

3. What does *Elohim* mean? What does *Yahweh* mean?

4. What does *imago Dei* refer to?

5. Describe the creation of humans found in Genesis 2.

6. List nine attributes of God.

7. Explain what transcendence and immanence mean.

CH 6

Study Guide *(continued)*

8. What are the three ways in which human beings bear God's image? Briefly explain each one.

9. What is stewardship? Give an example.

10. Describe God's plan for people as relational and sexed beings.

11. How is the biblical mandate of stewardship connected to our relationship with nature?

12. Briefly discuss seven truths in which the biblical creation story is distinct from other worldviews. Include the worldview idea that the creation story refutes.

13. What is the main belief of each of the following worldviews?
    Atheism:

    Pantheism:

    Nihilism:

    Gnosticism:

14. Read and study the five Key Verses listed at the top of the study guide.

7

Act 2: The Fall

Chapter 7 Syllabus

Lesson		Assignment		Page
1	In Class	REVIEW	Chapter 6 Test	
	In Class	DISCUSS	Questions for Chapter 7.1–7.2	128
	In Class	EXPLORE	Activity: News Analyses	129
	At Home	READ	Chapter 7.3–7.4	ST 94–96
	At Home	ANSWER	Questions for Chapter 7.3–7.4	130–131
2	In Class	DISCUSS	Questions for Chapter 7.3–7.4	
	In Class	EXPLORE	Activity: Breaking News Story	131
	At Home	READ	Chapter 7.5–7.6	ST 96–99
	At Home	ANSWER	Questions for Chapter 7.5–7.6	132–133
3	In Class	DISCUSS	Questions for Chapter 7.5–7.6	
	In Class	EXPLORE	Activity: Original Sin Scriptures	133–134
	At Home	READ	Chapter 7.7–7.8	ST 99–101
	At Home	ANSWER	Questions for Chapter 7.7–7.8	135–136
4	In Class	DISCUSS	Questions for Chapter 7.7–7.8	
	In Class	EXPLORE	Activity: Genesis 3:15 Study	136
	At Home	READ	Chapter 7.9–7.10	ST 101–104
	At Home	ANSWER	Questions for Chapter 7.9–7.10	137–138
5	In Class	DISCUSS	Questions for Chapter 7.9–7.10	
	In Class	EXPLORE	Activities: Student Covenant	138
6	In Class	EXPLORE	Activity: The Fall Charades	
7	In Class	WATCH	Videos	
	In Class	ANSWER	Video Questions	139–140
	In Class	DISCUSS	Video Questions	
8	In Class	EXPLORE	Activity: The Fall in Literature	141
	In Class	REVIEW FOR	Chapter 7 Test	142
9	In Class	STUDY FOR	Chapter 7 Test	
	In Class	ANSWER	Study Guide Questions	143–145
10	In Class	TAKE	Chapter 7 Test	
	At Home	READ	Chapter 8.1–8.2	ST 105–108
	At Home	ANSWER	Questions for Chapter 8.1–8.2	148–149

*Student Textbook (ST) Student Manual (SM)

CH 7

Chapter 7.1–7.2

DISCUSSION QUESTIONS

1. What is *shalom?* [7.1]

2. What would you say is wrong with the world now? What is the main problem? [7.1]

3. What ideas come into your mind when you hear the word *sin*? [7.2]

4. Describe sin, transgression, and iniquity—three of the words for wrongdoing in the Bible. [7.2]

Activity

NEWS ANALYSES

OBJECTIVE:

You will analyze news stories, classifying them according to the type of sin they represent and the type of relationship they impact.

PREPARATION:

- Materials needed: computer, paper, and pen
- Time required: 20–25 minutes

PROCEDURE:

1. Your teacher will divide the class into four groups and assign each group one of four relationships: God, ourselves, other people, and creation.
2. Use computers to search online for news stories. Find a news story that shows sin, transgression, or iniquity related to your assigned relationship.
3. Read the article and summarize how the sin affects the relationship assigned to you. You will have 10–12 minutes for this step.
4. Each group will present its findings to the class.

CH 7

Chapter 7.3–7.4

DISCUSSION QUESTIONS

1. What was the first sin? How was it more than breaking a rule? [7.3]

2. How did the serpent tempt Eve? How does Satan tempt people to sin? [7.3]

3. Do you think it was wrong for Adam and Eve to seek independence from God? Why or why not? [7.3]

4. Is death natural or unnatural? Explain. [7.4]

5. What is spiritual death? [7.4]

6. How has humanity's relationship with God been fractured? What evidence do you see of this in the world today? [7.4]

7. How has humanity's relationship with nature been fractured? What evidence do you see of this in the world today? [7.4]

Activity

BREAKING NEWS STORY

OBJECTIVE:

You will create a skit of a breaking news story about the fall.

PREPARATION:

- Materials needed: none
- Time required: 15–20 minutes

PROCEDURE:

1. Your group will brainstorm how to present the fall as breaking news in a newscast. Then your group will create a skit. Choose who will report or take turns reporting. Then, rehearse the skit.
2. Your group will present its news story skit to the class. You and your classmates will discuss the most effective points made in the presentations.

CH 7

Chapter 7.5–7.6

DISCUSSION QUESTIONS

1. How has every person's relationship with his or her own self been fractured? What evidence do you see of this in the world today? [7.5]

2. How have people's relationships with others been broken or fractured? What evidence do you see of this in the world today? [7.5]

3. Christopher Hitchens, an atheist, said: "Once you assume a creator and a plan, it makes us objects in a cruel experiment whereby we are created sick and commanded to be well." How might you respond to his statement? [7.6]

4. What is the doctrine of original sin? [7.6]

5. Are humans basically good or evil? Explain. [7.6]

Activity

ORIGINAL SIN SCRIPTURES

OBJECTIVE:

You will discuss and note observations in Bible verses related to the doctrine of original sin.

PREPARATION:

- Materials needed: Bible and pen
- Time required: 15–20 minutes

PROCEDURE:

1. Your student textbook cited the following Bible verses: Romans 3:9–26, 5:12, Jeremiah 17:9, Psalm 14:1–3. These verses support the concept of human sinfulness and the doctrine of original sin—that is, the belief that Adam and Eve's first sin corrupted the nature of their descendants, including us! But there are many more verses in Scripture on these topics.
2. Work with a partner to find and discuss each passage listed in the study on the following page. Spend 2–3 minutes on each verse. Take brief notes on what you discuss and observe in each verse.
3. Be ready to share your discussion notes and observations with the class.

Activity | BIBLE VERSES ABOUT ORIGINAL SIN STUDY

Job 14:4, 15:14–16

Psalm 51:5

Isaiah 53:6, 64:6

Mark 7:14–23

Ephesians 2:1–3

1 John 1:8–10

Chapter 7.7–7.8

DISCUSSION QUESTIONS

1. Why did God ask Adam where he was? Where was Eve? How did Adam and Eve respond to God? [7.7]

2. What is the protoevangelium and what does it say about God's character? [7.7]

3. How might physical death be seen as gracious? [7.7]

4. How do you think Eve felt when Cain was born? Why? [7.8]

5. What were Cain's sins? [7.8]

CH 7

7.7–7.8 *(continued)*

6. What is the way of Cain, and how does it contrast with those who walked with God? Give examples of people who walked in each path. [7.8]

7. What did God decide to do because most people followed the way of Cain? [7.8]

8. Why is faith necessary to please God? [7.8]

Activity

GENESIS 3:15 STUDY

OBJECTIVE:
You will analyze the relationship between Genesis 3:15 and other verses of Scripture.

PREPARATION:
- Materials needed: TR 7.4A, Bible and pen
- Time required: 20–25 minutes

PROCEDURE:
1. Use your Bible to complete the TR 7.4A Genesis 3:15 Study.
2. Be ready to share your answers.

Chapter 7.9–7.10

DISCUSSION QUESTIONS

1. What is a covenant? How does it differ from a contract? [7.9]

2. Describe God's covenant with Noah and the sign God gave for that covenant. [7.9]

3. What is significant about God's covenant with Noah? [7.9]

4. Why was God opposed to the tower of Babel? [7.9]

CH 7 7.9–7.10 *(continued)*

5. What did God do to prevent people from completing the tower? What happened as a result of God's action? [7.9]

6. Why didn't God abandon people when they sinned? What does this mean for us today? [7.10]

Activity

STUDENT COVENANT

OBJECTIVE:

You will draft a covenant to reinforce the concept that a covenant is an agreement between two parties that involves both rights and responsibilities.

PREPARATION:

- Materials needed: PS 7.5A, paper, and pen
- Time required: 25–30 minutes

PROCEDURE:

1. Follow along as your teacher displays PS 7.5A Student Covenant.
2. Your teacher will divide the class into groups of four or five students to work for 10 minutes to develop a one-page draft of a student covenant.
3. Be prepared to share items from your draft.
4. Vote on the items in order to develop a final draft as a class. The items chosen will be written on the board.

Videos

DISCUSSION QUESTIONS

Read the discussion questions before each video is played so you know what to listen for.

Video 1: What Is Sin, and Why Does It Matter?

1. How does the speaker explain the concept of sin?

2. What does the speaker mean when he says that human beings have "a moral machine" built into them? What does he say supports this claim?

3. What dimension does sin add to the concept of wrongdoing?

4. What is guilt?

5. Why are people willing to admit that there is right and wrong but don't like to use the term *sin*?

Video 2: Is It a Sin to Have Doubt?

1. The speaker had a misconception about asking questions, sin, and doubt. What was it?

2. What realization helped the speaker to see he was mistaken?

3. What three recommendations does the speaker give for dealing with doubt?

4. Who were the Bereans, and what did they teach us?

5. How is the Bible unique compared to the thousands of religious books the speaker read?

CH 7

Videos (continued)

Video 3: What Is a Covenant?

1. What is another word for *covenant?*

2. What are the five parts of ancient covenants or treaties?

3. What example does the speaker give of a treaty or covenant in the Bible?

4. Does the covenant with Noah have the five parts that the speaker describes are characteristic of a covenant or treaty? Explain.

Video 4: Is the Bible Restrictive?

1. Why is it not a good idea to push back against the restrictions that God places upon us?

2. What illustration does the speaker give to discuss this?

3. Many people object to God's restrictions, especially about sex. They want to be free to disobey them. What does the speaker say they need to keep in mind?

4. What is an ironic result of sin?

Activity

THE FALL IN LITERATURE

OBJECTIVE:

You will research famous works inspired by the fall of Adam and Eve.

PREPARATION:

- Materials needed: computer, paper, and pen
- Time required: 20–30 minutes

PROCEDURE:

1. Your teacher will divide the class into groups.

2. Your group will be assigned one of the following works:

Group 1: *The Life of Adam and Eve* (also called the *Apocalypse of Moses*), apocryphal work

Group 2: *Le Jeu d'Adam* (also called *The Play of Adam* or *The Mystery of Adam*), author unknown, medieval religious drama

Group 3: *Paradise Lost*, by John Milton, epic poem

Group 4: *The Diaries of Adam and Eve*, by Mark Twain, a short story later adapted into a play

Group 5: *Perelandra*, by C. S. Lewis, science fiction novel

3. You will have 12 minutes to research the work you were assigned. See what you can learn about the origin of the work (Groups 1 and 2), or the author (Groups 3–5), as well as the work's plot and purpose (all groups).

4. Be ready to present the results of your research to the class.

CH 7

Chapter 7 Review

Take notes during the slide presentation.

Chapter 7 Study Guide

Key Terms

shalom
sin
transgression
iniquity
the fall
doctrine of original sin
covenant

Key Verses

Genesis 3:6
Genesis 3:14–19
Genesis 9:7–13
Romans 3:23
Romans 5:12

1. Describe God's creation and the four relationships at the beginning of creation.

2. Is the way the world was upon creation the way our world is today? What do non-Christians think? What does the Christian worldview say?

3. What is the most common word used in the Bible for wrongdoing, and what does it mean? What are two other words used in the Bible for wrongdoing, and what do they mean?

4. Name and describe the second act in the Bible's metanarrative.

5. How did the physical and spiritual consequences of the fall affect people's relationship with God? How do those consequences continue today?

CH 7 Study Guide *(continued)*

6. How did the fall affect nature and people's relationship with it?

7. How did the fall affect how Adam and Eve and the rest of humanity see themselves?

8. How did the fall affect Adam and Eve's relationship and all human relationships ever since?

9. Who or what do some secularists and atheists blame for evil in the world? How might Christians respond to their accusations?

10. What is the doctrine of original sin, and why should we care about it today?

11. In what three ways did God show grace to Adam and Eve after they ate the fruit of the Tree of Knowledge of Good and Evil?

12. Explain who Cain, Abel, and Seth were; what they did; and how God interacted with them.

13. Who were Enoch and Lamech? What two paths did humans begin to follow? What did God decide to do when people filled the world with sin?

14. According to the Bible, what does a rainbow signify? Include and define the term *covenant* in your answer.

15. Did the flood stop people from sinning? What happened with the tower of Babel? Explain.

16. Why should we have hope despite the fall, knowing that sin and death are all around us?

17. Read and study the five Key Verses listed at the top of the study guide.

8

Act 3: Redemption Initiated—Israel

Act 3: Redemption Initiated—Israel

Chapter 8 Syllabus

Lesson		Assignment		Page
1	In Class	REVIEW	Chapter 7 Test	
	In Class	DISCUSS	Questions for Chapter 8.1–8.2	148–149
	In Class	EXPLORE	Activity: Family Lines	149
	At Home	READ	Chapter 8.3–8.4	ST 108–110
	At Home	ANSWER	Questions for Chapter 8.3–8.4	150–151
2	In Class	DISCUSS	Questions for Chapter 8.3–8.4	
	In Class	EXPLORE	Activity: Law Codes	151
	At Home	READ	Chapter 8.5–8.6	ST 110–113
	At Home	ANSWER	Questions for Chapter 8.5–8.6	152–153
3	In Class	DISCUSS	Questions for Chapter 8.5–8.6	
	In Class	EXPLORE	Activity: Actions Have Consequences	153
	At Home	READ	Chapter 8.7–8.8	ST 113–115
	At Home	ANSWER	Questions for Chapter 8.7–8.8	154–155
4	In Class	DISCUSS	Questions for Chapter 8.7–8.8	
	In Class	EXPLORE	Activity: Faith Under Pressure	155
	At Home	READ	Chapter 8.9–8.10	ST 115–119
	At Home	ANSWER	Questions for Chapter 8.9–8.10	156–157
5	In Class	DISCUSS	Questions for Chapter 8.9–8.10	
	In Class	EXPLORE	Activity: God Keeps His Promises	157
6	In Class	EXPLORE	Activity: What's My Name?	
7	In Class	WATCH	Videos	
	In Class	ANSWER	Video Questions	158–159
	In Class	DISCUSS	Video Questions	
8	In Class	EXPLORE	Activity: Finding Jesus in the Festivals	160
	In Class	REVIEW FOR	Chapter 8 Test	161
9	In Class	STUDY FOR	Chapter 8 Test	
	In Class	ANSWER	Study Guide Questions	162–163
10	In Class	TAKE	Chapter 8 Test	
	At Home	READ	Chapter 9.1–9.2	ST 120–123
	At Home	ANSWER	Questions for Chapter 9.1–9.2	166–167

*Student Textbook (ST) Student Manual (SM)

CH 8 Chapter 8.1–8.2

DISCUSSION QUESTIONS

1. What was God's goal in blessing Abraham and his family? [8.1]

2. What did Joseph mean when he said, "You meant evil against me, but God meant it for good"? What does this say about how God accomplishes his purposes? [8.1]

3. What does the name I AM mean? In what way would this name have been significant for Moses and the Israelites? [8.2]

4. How is the covenant God made with the people of Israel similar to the covenant God made with Abraham? [8.2]

5. Based on what you learned about Moses in the story of Israel and the exodus, does God only use perfect people to accomplish his purposes? Explain.

6. What was the purpose of the laws and commandments God gave?

Activity

FAMILY LINES

OBJECTIVE:

You will diagram a family tree tracing the covenant promises to Abraham's family.

PREPARATION:

- Materials needed: Bible, white printer paper, and pen
- Time required: 15–20 minutes

PROCEDURE:

1. Work with a partner. Use a piece of white printer paper to diagram a family tree showing the family of Abraham mentioned in Chapter 8.1. You may use your Bible to look up details such as the names of Jacob's sons.
2. Indicate the members of the family tree who were chosen to carry on the covenant promises by placing an *X* next to the names of those who were not included in the covenant promises. Remember that although those with the *X* beside their names were blessed by Abraham's family (see Genesis 12:2–3, 18:18; Galatians 3:8), they were not given the specific responsibilities and blessings that came with God's promises and covenant with Israel.
3. Place Jesus' name on the family tree. You do not need to include the genealogy of Jesus, although you are welcome to include it if you wish and if time permits. If you name the twelve sons of Jacob on the tree, Jesus should be connected to the tribe of Judah.
4. Write *Promise given* next to Abraham's name and *Promise fulfilled* next to Jesus' name.

CH 8

Chapter 8.3–8.4

DISCUSSION QUESTIONS

1. What was the purpose of the tabernacle? [8.3]

2. What was the purpose of the laws, sacrifices, and festivals in the Old Testament? [8.3]

3. Why are most of these laws, sacrifices, and festivals no longer observed by Christians today? [8.3]

4. Why did God command the Israelites to drive out the Canaanites? [8.4]

5. What is significant about the story of Ruth? [8.4]

6. Why did Israel keep repeating their destructive pattern during the time of the judges? Do we have similar tendencies today?

Activity

LAW CODES

OBJECTIVE:

You will decode terms that represent the laws, sacrifices, and festivals and match them to their descriptions.

PREPARATION:

- Materials needed: TR 8.2A and pencil
- Time required: 15–20 minutes

PROCEDURE:

1. Obtain a copy of TR 8.2A Law Codes. Decode the terms and match them with their descriptions.
2. Check your answers with your teacher.
3. Answer the question at the bottom of the page and share your response with the class.

CH 8

Chapter 8.5–8.6

DISCUSSION QUESTIONS

1. What did the first three kings of Israel have in common? What choices created different endings to their personal stories? [8.5]

2. What was the covenant God made with David? How does it compare to the covenant God made with Abraham and the Israelites? [8.5]

3. Describe the history of the northern kingdom. [8.6]

4. What role did Elijah and Elisha play in the history of the northern kingdom? [8.6]

5. Why do you think Elijah challenged the prophets of Baal to a contest, and was this effective? [8.6]

6. How did the healing of Naaman from leprosy relate to Israel's mission? [8.6]

7. Why did God send Israel into exile? [8.6]

Activity

ACTIONS HAVE CONSEQUENCES

OBJECTIVE:

You will connect the actions of the early Israelites with the consequences of those actions.

PREPARATION:

- Materials needed: TR 8.3A
- Time required: 15–20 minutes

PROCEDURE:

1. Take one action card and one consequence card from TR 8.3A Actions Have Consequences. Do not show them to the other students.
2. Stand up as your teacher directs. If your teacher calls on you, read your action card aloud. If another student is reading an action card, look at your consequences card to see if it matches the action card. If your consequence card matches the action card that was read, you should say, "There will be consequences!" and go stand next to the person who read the action card.
3. Another student will then read an action card and the process will repeat. The game is over when all students are connected by linking pinky fingers.
4. If time permits, reshuffle the cards and play again.

CH 8

Chapter 8.7–8.8

DISCUSSION QUESTIONS

1. Describe the history of the southern kingdom. [8.7]

2. How were Jehoshaphat, Hezekiah, and Josiah different from the kings of the northern kingdom? [8.7]

3. How did Daniel and his friends remain faithful to God in exile? [8.8]

4. How do you think Christians today should live in a non-Christian culture? [8.8]

5. What do Daniel's visions about the future reveal? [8.8]

Activity

FAITH UNDER PRESSURE

OBJECTIVE:

You will write a paragraph reflecting on faithfulness to God in a hostile culture.

PREPARATION:

- Materials needed: Bible, paper, and pen
- Time required: 20–30 minutes

PROCEDURE:

1. Choose one biblical character from the period of the exile who provided an example of faithfulness to God when pressured to conform to pagan culture. This character could be Daniel or another character mentioned in Chapter 8.8 or another biblical character living under a foreign government, such as Esther or Nehemiah.
2. Write a reflection paragraph answering the following questions:
    - What challenge did this biblical character face?
    - How did this biblical character respond to the challenge?
    - How did God engage in the story and what does that reveal about God's character?
    - What specific challenges do I face in the culture around me?
    - How can I relate to God like this biblical character did?
    - What aspect of God's character can I be encouraged by as I face the challenge to conform to culture?
3. Share your reflections with the class.

CH 8

Chapter 8.9–8.10

DISCUSSION QUESTIONS

1. What is the primary function of a biblical prophet? [8.9]

2. What things did the prophets condemn Israel for? How might the words of the prophets be relevant in our own time? [8.9]

3. What are some of the promises the prophets made to Israel? How might Christians today be encouraged by them? [8.9]

4. How would you summarize the storyline of the Old Testament so far? [8.10]

5. What is God like throughout Israel's history? What kind of God is he revealed to be? [8.10]

6. According to 2 Timothy 2:13, God is trustworthy and faithful. Describe a story or event discussed in Chapter 8 that supports this verse. [8.10]

Activity

GOD KEEPS HIS PROMISES

OBJECTIVE:

You will research Old Testament prophecies to find out where they are fulfilled or reaffirmed in later writings of the Bible.

PREPARATION:

- Materials needed: Bible, concordance or computer, paper, and pen
- Time required: 15–20 minutes

PROCEDURE:

1. Work with a partner to choose two of God's promises given by the prophets from the list below, and use a concordance or computer to find where that prophecy was fulfilled in the Bible. If the prophecy has not yet been fulfilled, check the New Testament for passages reaffirming that promise.
   - A coming king (Zechariah 9:9–13, 12:10–14)
   - The day of the Lord—God's judgment on the wicked (Zechariah 9:14–17, 12:1–9, 14:1–21; Malachi 4:1–3)
   - The restoration of Judah and Israel (Zechariah 10)
   - The coming of the Lord's messenger (Malachi 3:1–4, 4:5–6)
   - A new covenant (Jeremiah 31:31–34)
   - New hearts for God's people (Jeremiah 31:31–34)
   - The forgiveness of sin (Isaiah 53)
2. Write down your findings and present them to the class.

CH 8

Videos

DISCUSSION QUESTIONS

Read the discussion questions before each video is played so that you know what to listen for.

Video 1: What Role Does Religion Play in Society?

1. What is a religion?

2. Who is religious?

3. What do religions do in society?

4. According to the video, what does *shalom* mean and what does shalom look like in society?

5. What role did Jeremiah tell the Israelites to take while in exile? How does that relate to Christians today?

Video 2: Why So Many Rules?

1. How many rules are in the Old Testament?

2. According to Jewish tradition, why are there so many rules?

3. How were idols seen in the ancient world?

4. What is the parallel between children's need for many rules and the Israelites' need for extensive spiritual rules?

Video 3: Were Old Testament People Saved?

1. Could non-Israelites be saved since they weren't part of the chosen people?

2. Who was Naaman and what drove him to seek God?

3. Why wouldn't the prophet meet with Naaman?

4. Why didn't the prophet accept Naaman's gifts?

5. What actions of the prophet and what teachings of Jesus show us that non-Israelites could be saved?

CH 8

Activity

Activity

FINDING JESUS IN THE FESTIVALS

OBJECTIVE

You will discuss ways that Israel's festivals alluded to Christ or coincided with New Testament events.

PREPARATION:

- Materials needed: PS 8.8A and Bible
- Time required: 25–30 minutes

PROCEDURE:

1. Your teacher will display PS 8.8A Finding Jesus in the Festivals. Take turns reading the first three slides about the Feast of Tabernacles.
2. After you have finished reading the slides. Then, as a class, discusss any connections you see between the Old Testament festivals and New Testament Scriptures.
   Note: You may wish to reference your Bibles to examine these passages more closely during your small group discussion.
3. Take turns reading the information on the slides for the next festival and discuss. Continue until each festival has been discussed.

Chapter 8 Review

Take notes during the slide presentation.

CH 8

Chapter 8 Study Guide

Key Terms

Passover
tabernacle
Day of Atonement
temple
prophet

Key Verses

Genesis 50:20
Acts 13:22
2 Kings 5:15
Jeremiah 29:7

1. Explain God's covenant with Abraham. Who were the next two descendants who received the covenant blessing?

2. Relate the Passover to the exodus from Egypt.

3. Explain the purpose of the tabernacle.

4. Differentiate between the two categories of Old Testament laws, the two types of sacrifices, and the three major festivals.

5. Describe the pattern Israel fell into during the period of the the judges.

6. Explain why God told the Israelites to remove the Canaanites from the Promised Land.

7. Explain the purpose of the temple.

8. Give a brief description of the first three kings of Israel.

9. Describe the consequences of sin in the northern kingdom and how that sin interfered with Israel's mission.

10. Distinguish Jehoshaphat, Hezekiah, and Josiah from the other kings of Judah and Israel by indicating how they served the Lord.

11. Give examples of how Daniel, Shadrach, Meshach, and Abednego modeled faithfulness to God in exile.

12. What is a prophet, and what types of messages were they entrusted to deliver?

13. Read and study the four Key Verses listed at the beginning of the study guide.

9

Interlude—The Second Temple Period

Interlude—The Second Temple Period

Chapter 9 Syllabus

Lesson		Assignment		Page
1	In Class	REVIEW	Chapter 8 Test	
	In Class	DISCUSS	Questions for Chapter 9.1–9.2	166–167
	In Class	EXPLORE	Activity: Rise of Kingdoms	167
	At Home	READ	Chapter 9.3–9.4	ST 123–125
	At Home	ANSWER	Questions for Chapter 9.3–9.4	168
2	In Class	DISCUSS	Questions for Chapter 9.3–9.4	
	In Class	EXPLORE	Activity: Clash of Worldviews	169
	At Home	READ	Chapter 9.5–9.6	ST 125–128
	At Home	ANSWER	Questions for Chapter 9.5–9.6	170–171
3	In Class	DISCUSS	Questions for Chapter 9.5–9.6	
	In Class	EXPLORE	Activity: God-Tinted Glasses	171
	At Home	READ	Chapter 9.7–9.8	ST 128–130
	At Home	ANSWER	Questions for Chapter 9.7–9.8	172–173
4	In Class	DISCUSS	Questions for Chapter 9.7–9.8	
	In Class	EXPLORE	Activity: What To Do?	173
	At Home	READ	Chapter 9.9–9.10	ST 130–134
	At Home	ANSWER	Questions for Chapter 9.9–9.10	174
5	In Class	DISCUSS	Questions for Chapter 9.9–9.10	
	In Class	EXPLORE	Activity: Debating Factions Prep	175
6	In Class	EXPLORE	Activity: Debating Factions	
7	In Class	WATCH	Videos	
	In Class	ANSWER	Video Questions	176–177
	In Class	DISCUSS	Video Questions	
8	In Class	EXPLORE	Activity: Guess Who I Am	178
	In Class	REVIEW FOR	Chapter 9 Test	179
9	In Class	STUDY FOR	Chapter 9 Test	
	In Class	ANSWER	Complete Study Guide	180–181
10	In Class	TAKE	Chapter 9 Test	
	At Home	READ	Chapter 10.1–10.2	ST 135–138
	At Home	ANSWER	Questions for Chapter 10.1–10.2	184

*Student Textbook (ST) Student Manual (SM)

CH 9

Chapter 9.1–9.2

DISCUSSION QUESTIONS

1. Who or what are the four beasts in Daniel's vision? [9.1]

2. Why were Ezra and Nehemiah so zealous in their reforms? [9.1]

3. What is the difference between the intertestamental period and the second temple period? [9.2]

4. What is hellenization? How was it helpful and how was it harmful? [9.2]

5. How did Jews respond to the pressures of hellenization? [9.2]

Activity

RISE OF KINGDOMS

OBJECTIVE:

You will illustrate the four beasts described in Daniel 7 and the four kingdoms they represent.

PREPARATION:

- Materials needed: Bible, Bible commentary or computer, student textbook, white paper, and pen
- Time required: 20–30 minutes

PROCEDURE:

1. Work with a partner to draw pictures of the beasts described in Daniel's vision in Daniel 7.
2. Label each beast with the name of the kingdom it represents. Turn to Chapter 9.1–9.2 in your student textbook. List the biblical characters below the beast/kingdom they lived under.
3. If time permits, read Bible commentaries or use a computer to research the possible meanings of the beasts' attributes in Daniel 7. Use what you find to add additional labels or explanations to accompany your illustrations.

CH 9

Chapter 9.3–9.4

DISCUSSION QUESTIONS

1. How do the Maccabees compare with other Jewish leaders such as Daniel, Ezra, and Nehemiah? [9.3]

2. According to Matthew 21:1–17, what similarities do you see between the actions of Judah Maccabee and Jesus? How are they different? [9.3]

3. In what ways is Herod similar to the Pharaoh of the Exodus story (see Exodus 1)? [9.4]

4. What were the positives and negatives of Roman rule? [9.4]

Activity

CLASH OF WORLDVIEWS

OBJECTIVE:
You will compare the clash of hellenism and Judaism to present-day worldview conflicts.

PREPARATION:
- Materials needed: TR 9.2A, Bible, and pen
- Time required: 20–30 minutes

PROCEDURE:
1. Read the background information on TR 9.2A Clash of Worldviews.
2. Complete the analysis of ancient and modern worldviews.
3. Discuss your answers with the class.

CH 9

Chapter 9.5–9.6

DISCUSSION QUESTIONS

1. Why were the temple and the land so important to Jews? [9.5]

2. Why were the Torah and racial identity so important to Jews? [9.5]

3. What potential dangers might be associated with these Jewish symbols: temple, land, Torah, and racial identity? [9.5]

4. What was the purpose of the synagogue? [9.6]

5. Who were the Samaritans and why was there such animosity between them and the Jews? [9.6]

Activity

GOD-TINTED GLASSES

OBJECTIVE:

You will research biblical models for conflict resolution and overcoming prejudices.

PREPARATION:

- Materials needed: PS 9.3A, TR 9.3A, Bible, and pen
- Time required: 25–30 minutes

PROCEDURE:

1. Explore the positions and geographical significance of Galilee, Judea, and Samaria on the map displayed by your teacher.
2. Consider what the Jews and Samaritans did to avoid each other. Think about whether there are people in your life that you tend to avoid or treat differently due to conflicts, hurts, or prejudices.
3. Complete TR 9.3A God-Tinted Glasses. Be ready to discuss your answers with the class.

CH 9

Chapter 9.7–9.8

DISCUSSION QUESTIONS

1. Compare and contrast the Pharisees with the Sadducees. [9.7]

2. Compare and contrast the Essenes with the Zealots. [9.7]

3. What role did the books of the Apocrypha (such as *1–2 Maccabees*, *Susanna*, and *Tobit*) play in the life of Jews? [9.8]

4. What were some beliefs that arose or became prominent during the second temple period? [9.8]

5. How might stories encourage Christians today to remain faithful to God? [9.8]

Activity

WHAT TO DO?

OBJECTIVE:

You will create solutions for dilemmas that Jews living during the second temple period might have faced.

PREPARATION:

- Materials needed: TR 9.4A, Bible, paper, and pen
- Time required: 20–30 minutes

PROCEDURE:

1. Although stories from the second temple period encouraged Jews to avoid compromise and stay faithful to God, this was often easier said than done.
2. Work with your group to solve the dilemma from TR 9.4A Dilemmas that your teacher assigned you.
3. With your group, discuss whether there are any concepts from the Old Testament or second temple literature that provide guiding principles.
4. Present your dilemma and solution to the class.

CH 9

Chapter 9.9–9.10

DISCUSSION QUESTIONS

1. List five of the main hopes of the Jewish people during the second temple period. [9.9]

2. What kind of messiah did the Jews expect? How does that expectation compare with who Jesus was? [9.9]

3. What similarities do you see between modern times and the time of the second temple period? [9.10]

4. What are some of the messiah-like figures that people today look to in order to fix what is wrong with the world? Can any of these ultimately solve the world's problems? Explain. [9.10]

Activity

DEBATING FACTIONS PREP

OBJECTIVE:

You will prepare for a debate from the perspective of one of the four Jewish factions.

PREPARATION:

- Materials needed: reference books or computer, Bible, paper, and pen
- Time required: 25–30 minutes

PROCEDURE:

1. Use reference books, computers, and Bibles to study your faction's perspective on the topic you were assigned.
2. Prepare the debate points you want to make that represent your faction's perspective on the assigned topic, as well as possible rebuttals to opposing factions.

CH 9

Videos

DISCUSSION QUESTIONS

Read the discussion questions before each video is played so that you know what to listen for.

Video 1: What Happened between the Testaments?

1. How can we know what happened between the Old and New Testaments?

2. What major movement occurred among the Jewish leadership during the intertestamental period and how did the post-revolt leadership react to it?

3. What similar temptations do modern Christians face and how can they be overcome?

4. What is one thing that can help Christians think well and live well under pressure?

Video 2: Why Do Christians Believe Contradicting Views?

1. What does it mean to hold contradictory views?

2. Why do many people, including Christians, hold contradictory views?

3. What is the solution for helping Christians to think well and reject contradictory views?

Video 3: How Should Christians Interact with Culture?

1. What is a common but poorly constructed definition of "culture"?

2. What are two poor responses to culture?

3. What does the freedom God gave to humans allow for?

4. What does God call Christians to do?

Video 4: Can We Maintain Hope in a Broken Culture?

1. How should we make sense of the moment we live in?

2. What is Christian hope, and how can Christians maintain a sense of hope in this culture?

3. How can Christian hope be a bridge to people who are not Christians?

Video 5: How Can the Church Encourage Healthy Grieving?

1. How is the book of Psalms helpful for grieving?

2. What are two ways Christians can lament?

3. How can the church facilitate healthy grieving and lament?

Video 6: How Can Christians Begin to Engage with and Change the Culture?

1. Is it better to focus on changing the world or on changing our communities?

2. What are some ways each of us can focus on changing our own community?

CH 9

Activity

Activity

GUESS WHO I AM

OBJECTIVE

You will identify biblical characters from the second temple period based on nonverbal or verbal clues.

PREPARATION:

- Materials needed: TR 9.8A, box, textbook, and paper
- Time required: 25–30 minutes

PROCEDURE:

1. The class will be divided into two teams. Your teacher prepared a box with slips of paper from TR 9.8A Guess Who I Am. Take one from the box as it is passed around but do not show it to anyone else.
2. Look in your textbook for identifying actions, events, or characteristics of the biblical character on your slip of paper so you can give strong clues.
3. When it is your turn, go to the front of the classroom. You will have 20 seconds to pantomime actions representing your character while the other students on your team guess who your character is. If your team guesses correctly, it will receive three points.
4. If after 20 seconds no one guesses correctly, you have 30 more seconds to speak something your character might have said or retell part of that person's life through his or her eyes. However, do not say the name of the character or your team will not get any points. If your team guesses correctly, it will receive one point. If the guess is incorrect, the other team gets a chance to guess. If they answer correctly, that team will get one point. The team with the most points at the end wins the game.

Chapter 9 Review

Take notes during the slide presentation.

CH 9

Chapter 9 Study Guide

Key Terms

hellenization
Hanukkah
synagogue
Samaritans
Pharisees
Sadducees

Key Verses

Daniel 7:13–14
Acts 17:2–3
Galatians 4:4–5

1. What are the empires represented in Daniel's vision?

2. Give examples of the challenges Jews returning from exile faced.

3. Describe the rise of Greek culture during the second temple period.

4. Explain the factors that led to the Maccabean Revolt.

5. How did the Maccabee family get their name and what were they like as rulers?

6. Explain how the rise of the Roman Empire set the stage for the birth, life, and death of Christ.

7. What were the four key Jewish symbols during the second temple period.

8. Explain the role of synagogues post-exile.

9. How did Jews and Samaritans relate to one another?

10. Describe the Pharisees and Sadducees.

11. Describe the Essenes and Zealots.

12. Give examples of Jewish literature from the second temple period.

13. What were the the five hopes of the Jewish people during the second temple period?

14. Read and study the Key Verses listed at the beginning of the study guide.

10

Act 4: Redemption Accomplished—Jesus

Act 4: Redemption Accomplished—Jesus

Chapter 10 Syllabus

Lesson		Assignment		Page
1	In Class	REVIEW	Chapter 9 Test	
	In Class	DISCUSS	Questions for Chapter 10.1–10.2	184
	In Class	EXPLORE	Activity: Symbolic Numbers	185
	At Home	READ	Chapter 10.3–10.4	ST 138–140
	At Home	ANSWER	Questions for Chapter 10.3–10.4	186
2	In Class	DISCUSS	Questions for Chapter 10.3–10.4	
	In Class	EXPLORE	Activity: Pen a Parable	187
	At Home	READ	Chapter 10.5–10.6	ST 140–143
	At Home	ANSWER	Questions for Chapter 10.5–10.6	188
3	In Class	DISCUSS	Questions for Chapter 10.5–10.6	
	In Class	EXPLORE	Activity: Identifying Jesus	189
	At Home	READ	Chapter 10.7–10.8	ST 143–145
	At Home	ANSWER	Questions for Chapter 10.7–10.8	190
4	In Class	DISCUSS	Questions for Chapter 10.7–10.8	
	In Class	EXPLORE	Activity: Teach Others Also	191
	At Home	READ	Chapter 10.9–10.10	ST 146–148
	At Home	ANSWER	Questions for Chapter 10.9–10.10	192
5	In Class	DISCUSS	Questions for Chapter 10.9–10.10	
	In Class	EXPLORE	Activity: The Incarnation Bible Study	193
6	In Class	EXPLORE	Activity: First-Century Sleuth	
7	In Class	WATCH	Videos	
	In Class	ANSWER	Video Questions	194–196
	In Class	DISCUSS	Video Questions	
8	In Class	EXPLORE	Activity: Mythical or Factual?	197
	In Class	REVIEW FOR	Chapter 10 Test	198
9	In Class	STUDY FOR	Chapter 10 Test	
	In Class	ANSWER	Complete Study Guide	199–201
10	In Class	TAKE	Chapter 10 Test	
	At Home	READ	Chapter 11.1–11.2	ST 149–152
	At Home	ANSWER	Questions for Chapter 11.1–11.2	204–205

*Student Textbook (ST) Student Manual (SM)

CH 10 Chapter 10.1–10.2

DISCUSSION QUESTIONS

1. What is the Incarnation, and what makes it significant? [10.1]

2. Why is the Incarnation necessary for salvation? [10.1]

3. "When Jesus became human, this confirmed that our problem is not that we are human, but that we are not human enough." Based on what you know of the biblical story so far, what do you think this statement means? [10.1]

4. What is the kingdom of God? Why would Jewish people in the first century be excited by the message, "The kingdom of God is at hand"? [10.2]

Activity

SYMBOLIC NUMBERS

OBJECTIVE:

You will articulate how symbolic numbers in the Bible reinforce its message.

PREPARATION:

- Materials needed: Bible, pen, and paper
- Time required: 20–25 minutes

PROCEDURE:

1. Work with your group to find symbolic numbers represented in your assigned Bible passage. Use the information about biblical numbers below and discuss how the numbers reinforce the story or message in the passage.
   - The number one symbolizes the unity of God and the singular sacrifice of Christ.
   - The number three symbolizes the triune nature of God and completeness.
   - The number four symbolizes the creative work of God and universal truth.
   - The number seven symbolizes completion, perfection, and rest.
   - The number eight symbolizes new life, resurrection, a new covenant, and new beginnings.
   - The number twelve symbolizes God's government.
   - The number forty symbolizes testing and trials.[1]
2. Have a representative briefly report your group's findings to the class.

[1]Chilton, Brian G., "Reference Guide to Biblical Numerology," Cross Examined, https://crossexamined.org/reference-guide-biblical-numerology/.

CH 10 Chapter 10.3–10.4

DISCUSSION QUESTIONS

1. What are common ideas about Jesus' identity. How did he identify himself? [10.3]

2. As the Messiah, what three roles did Jesus identify with? How did Jesus live out these roles? [10.3]

3. Why did Jesus teach in parables, knowing that parables would hide the truth from some people? [10.4]

4. What four things do Jesus' parables in Mark 4 and Matthew 13 teach about the kingdom of God? How was the nature of Jesus' kingdom different than the one his hearers were expecting? [10.4]

Activity

PEN A PARABLE

OBJECTIVE:

You will write a parable to explain a biblical truth.

PREPARATION:

- Materials needed: Bible, pen, and paper
- Time required: 20–25 minutes

PROCEDURE:

1. Work with a partner. Read Galatians 1:6–10. Write a parable demonstrating the foolishness of exchanging the gospel of Christ for a false gospel. Make sure the parable is unique. (A parable is a story in which characters acting in everyday situations represent a biblical truth.)
2. Share your parable with the class.

CH 10 Chapter 10.5–10.6

DISCUSSION QUESTIONS

1. What was the purpose of Jesus' miracles? [10.5]

2. Why do you think Jesus wept for Lazarus since he knew he was going to raise him from the dead? [10.5]

3. How did Jesus intensify the Old Testament commands? [10.6]

4. What did Jesus mean when he said, "Judge not, that you be not judged" (Matthew 7:1)? [10.6]

Activity

IDENTIFYING JESUS

OBJECTIVE:
You will use biblical and non-biblical evidence to rebut false claims about Jesus' identity.

PREPARATION:
- Materials needed: TR 10.3A and pen
- Time required: 25–30 minutes

PROCEDURE:
1. Read the directions for TR 10.3A Who Do You Say I Am? and write the number of the false belief next to the counter evidence that refutes it. There may be more than one answer next to each counterevidence statement.
2. Go over the answers before continuing with the activity.
3. Role play conversations about the identity of Jesus. Your teacher will play the part of a skeptic or member of a non-Christian religion. You and your classmates will take turns playing the part of a Christian. You may reference the counterevidence on TR 10.3A and your Bible to help you navigate the conversation.
4. The Christian should begin the conversation by asking the teacher, the skeptic, "Who do you think Jesus is?" Once the teacher responds, the Christian should ask clarifying questions and respectfully explain why the evidence supports a different conclusion about Jesus. Examples of clarifying questions are "What do you mean by ___________?" and "How did you come to believe that is true?" Such questions are helpful in navigating spiritual conversations with non-Christians.

CH 10

Chapter 10.7–10.8

DISCUSSION QUESTIONS

1. What is ironic about the Roman sign placed above Jesus' head, "This is Jesus, the King of the Jews"? [10.7]

2. What did Jesus accomplish on the cross? [10.7]

3. What are the alternative explanations of the resurrection? Are these alternatives plausible? Explain. [10.8]

4. The apostle Paul said that if Jesus didn't rise from the dead, our faith is worthless (1 Corinthians 15:17). Why is this the case? [10.8]

Activity

TEACH OTHERS ALSO

OBJECTIVE:

You will create a teaching aid to explain the gospel.

PREPARATION:

- Materials needed: pen and paper
- Time required: 10–15 minutes

PROCEDURE:

1. Create an illustration, acronym, or acrostic to explain the gospel message to someone who has never heard it before. Elements should include: what's wrong with the world, how Jesus overcame it, why we need Jesus, how we can be in right relationship with God, and why it's important. The teaching aid should use simple language and avoid Christian jargon.
2. If time allows, share your teaching aid with the class or role play using your teaching aid to share the gospel.

CH 10

Chapter 10.9–10.10

DISCUSSION QUESTIONS

1. What was Jesus' last command to his followers before his ascension, and why is it significant today? [10.9]

2. Name two major implications of the ascension of Jesus. [10.9]

3. What does it mean to have faith in Jesus? [10.10]

Activity

THE INCARNATION BIBLE STUDY

OBJECTIVE:
You will investigate God's Word on the correlation between the Incarnation of Jesus and the goodness of the body.

PREPARATION:
- Materials needed: TR 10.5A, Bible, and pen
- Time required: 25–30 minutes

PROCEDURE:
1. Read the instructions in TR 10.5A The Incarnation Bible Study and complete the exercise. Relate the Incarnation and other teachings of the New Testament to modern cultural issues regarding the human body.
2. If time allows, discuss your answers with the class.

CH 10

Videos

DISCUSSION QUESTIONS

Read the discussion questions before each video is played so that you know what to listen for.

▶ Video 1: Was Jesus Just a Magician?

1. What is a magician?

2. How is the feeding of the 5,000 from a few loaves and fish different from magic tricks?

3. What is the evidence for Jesus' death and resurrection?

4. What are three reasons people tell lies? Does this fit the disciples' situation?

5. What act demonstrates that Jesus was not a magician and was more than a man?

▶ Video 2: Did Jesus Claim to Be God?

1. How is Jesus different from other religious leaders or sages like Bahaullah?

2. How would you respond to someone who says Jesus never made explicit claims to be God?

3. How does Jesus' choice of words in the Gospels differentiate him from the prophets?

Video 3: Can Miracles Happen?

1. What is a miracle?

2. Can the Being who created natural laws overpower natural laws?

3. What is the greatest miracle in the Bible?

Video 4: What Is God's Kingdom?

1. What was the problem with Israel asking for a king?

2. How is the new covenant different from the old covenant?

3. How should Christians view their citizenship?

4. How should Christians see the role of local churches and local Christians?

5. What does it mean to live as a citizen of the kingdom of God?

CH 10

Videos (continued)

Video 5: Should Christians Judge Others?

1. What is the biggest lie or cliché about Christianity?

2. How is the belief that you shouldn't judge self-refuting?

3. What is the biblical view of judging?

4. How do we judge something properly?

Activity

MYTHICAL OR FACTUAL?

OBJECTIVE

You will be able to differentiate between the gospel accounts of Jesus' life and pagan mythologies.

PREPARATION:

- Materials needed: PS 10.8A
- Time required: 20–25 minutes

PROCEDURE:

1. Follow along as your teacher shows PS 10.8A Mythical or Factual? Read the claims made by skeptics about Jesus, then compare the details of Jesus' life with the details of two ancient mythologies.
2. When your teacher calls out, "Same!" raise your hand if you think the mythological account is similar enough to the life of Jesus to be concerned that Christians borrowed from it. When your teacher calls out, "Different!" raise your hand if you think that the mythical account is significantly different from the New Testament accounts of Jesus' life.
3. If time allows, consider with your class what you could say to someone who makes these kinds of claims. Also discuss whether you have seen or heard similar skeptical claims before.

CH 10

Chapter 10 Review

Take notes during the slide presentation.

Chapter 10 Study Guide

Key Terms
Incarnation
kingdom of God
gospel
redemption
ascension

Key Verses
Luke 1:26–33
Luke 4:17–19
John 1:14
1 Corinthians 15:3–4

1. Explain the three ways the Incarnation is significant.

2. How does Jesus' ministry relate to the gospel and the kingdom of God?

3. Contrast popular views of Jesus' identity with Jesus' own claim to be the Messiah.

4. Name three roles entailed in Jesus' position of Messiah.

5. List four lessons Jesus taught about the kingdom of God through parables.

6. Summarize the parable about the vineyard. Why did this parable upset the religious leaders?

7. Describe two miracles Jesus accomplished and what they were a sign of.

CH 10 Study Guide *(continued)*

8. Briefly describe the eight categories of people that Jesus referred to as blessed in the beatitudes.

9. Summarize the ethical teachings of the Sermon on the Mount.

10. Explain two aspects of Jesus' redemptive work on the cross.

11. What are three skeptical objections to the resurrection? Give a response to each one.

12. Give the most plausible explanation for the disciples' transformation.

13. Discuss two major implications of Jesus' ascension.

14. What did Jesus commission his disciples to do?

15. What is the meaning of the term *the Christ?*

16. What two titles did Jesus use for himself that show he claimed to be God?

17. What is the Golden Rule?

18. Explain Jesus' humanity and divinity.

19. Do the four Gospels agree on the divinity of Christ? How much of each Gospel is devoted to the crucifixion?

20. Is God concerned with outward actions, the heart, or both? Explain.

21. What did Jesus' birth fulfill for Israel?

22. Read and study the four Key Verses listed at the beginning of the study guide.

11

Act 5: Restoration Initiated—The Church

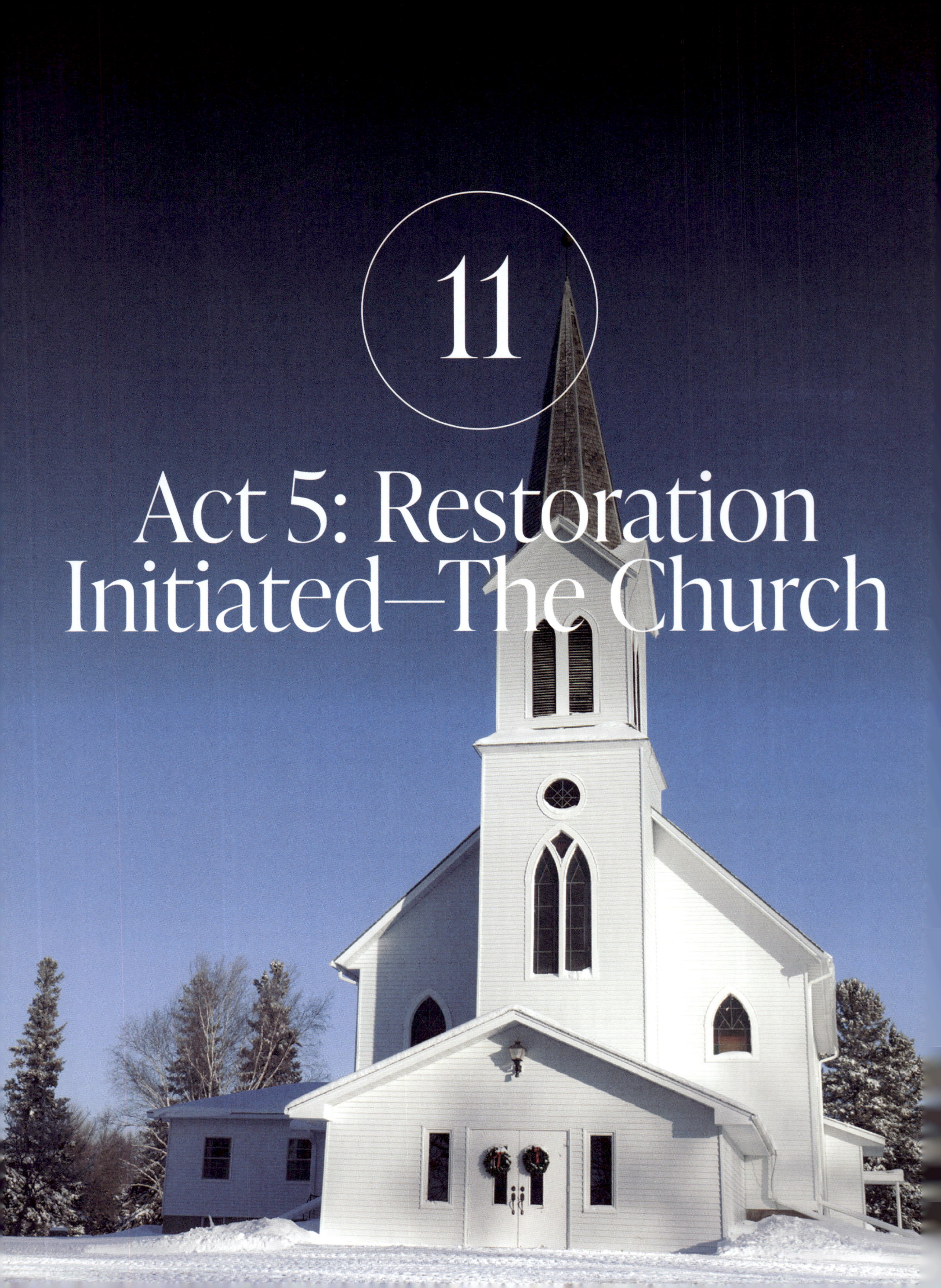

Act 5: Restoration Initiated—The Church

Chapter 11 Syllabus

Lesson		Assignment		Page
1	In Class	REVIEW	Chapter 10 Test	
	In Class	DISCUSS	Questions for Chapter 11.1–11.2	204–205
	In Class	EXPLORE	Activity: Church Comparisons	205
	At Home	READ	Chapter 11.3–11.4	ST 152–154
	At Home	ANSWER	Questions for Chapter 11.3–11.4	206–207
2	In Class	DISCUSS	Questions for Chapter 11.3–11.4	
	In Class	EXPLORE	Activity: Extraordinary Epistles	207
	At Home	READ	Chapter 11.5–11.6	ST 154–157
	At Home	ANSWER	Questions for Chapter 11.5–11.6	208–209
3	In Class	DISCUSS	Questions for Chapter 11.5–11.6	
	In Class	EXPLORE	Activity: Find Your Match	209
	At Home	READ	Chapter 11.7–11.8	ST 157–159
	At Home	ANSWER	Questions for Chapter 11.7–11.8	210–211
4	In Class	DISCUSS	Questions for Chapter 11.7–11.8	
	In Class	EXPLORE	Activity: Restoration Roundup	211
	At Home	READ	Chapter 11.9–11.10	ST 159–161
	At Home	ANSWER	Questions for Chapter 11.9–11.10	212–213
5	In Class	DISCUSS	Questions for Chapter 11.9–11.10	
	In Class	EXPLORE	Activity: Green Glossary	213
6	In Class	EXPLORE	Activity: The Ideal Church	214
7	In Class	WATCH	Videos	
	In Class	ANSWER	Video Questions	215–216
	In Class	DISCUSS	Video Questions	
8	In Class	EXPLORE	Activity: How Christianity Grew	217
	In Class	REVIEW FOR	Chapter 11 Test	218
9	In Class	STUDY FOR	Chapter 11 Test	
	In Class	ANSWER	Study Guide Questions	219–221
10	In Class	TAKE	Chapter 11 Test	
	At Home	READ	Chapter 12.1–12.2	ST 162–165
	At Home	ANSWER	Questions for Chapter 12.1–12.2	224

*Student Textbook (ST) Student Manual (SM)

CH 11

Chapter 11.1–11.2

DISCUSSION QUESTIONS

1. What did Jesus accomplish while he was on Earth? How did he do this? [11.1]

2. What does it mean that the kingdom of God is already here, but not yet? [11.1]

3. What is the church? What is the Great Commission? What is the relationship between the church and the Great Commission? [11.2]

4. What was Pentecost? What happened on that day that mattered to the followers of Jesus? [11.2]

5. How did early Christian communities testify to the transformative power of the gospel? [11.2]

Activity

CHURCH COMPARISONS

OBJECTIVE:

You will analyze five biblical metaphors that describe the church.

PREPARATION:

- Materials needed: Bible
- Time required: 20–25 minutes

PROCEDURE:

1. Your teacher will divide the class into five groups.
2. Each group will be assigned a set of Bible verses:
   - Group 1: Romans 12:4–5, 1 Corinthians 12:12–26, Ephesians 1:22–23
   - Group 2: 1 Corinthians 3:16–17, 2 Corinthians 6:14–18, Ephesians 2:19–22
   - Group 3: Ephesians 5:31–32; Revelation 19:6–8, 21:9
   - Group 4: 1 Peter 2:4–9; Revelation 1:4–6, 5:9–10
   - Group 5: Matthew 12:49–50, John 1:11–13, Galatians 3:26–29
3. Read and discuss your assigned verses to determine what the biblical metaphor teaches about the church.
4. Be ready to present your conclusions to the class.

CH 11

Chapter 11.3–11.4

DISCUSSION QUESTIONS

1. Why do you think Jesus' disciples experienced persecution from Jewish leaders? [11.3]

2. Where did Jesus' followers preach the gospel? [11.3]

3. What features of the Roman empire helped the gospel spread? [11.3]

4. What did Paul teach was the mystery, hidden before Christ's coming, that was revealed in the church? [11.4]

5. How did the apostles address the conflict between Jews and Gentiles? [11.4]

6. The apostles taught that the gospel makes a difference in all of our relationships. Think about your relationship with your parents or your teachers. How might the gospel make a difference in how you behave in those relationships? [11.4]

7. What behaviors should characterize a Christian's life? [11.4]

Activity

EXTRAORDINARY EPISTLES

OBJECTIVE:

You will compose an epistle addressing pressing issues in the church today.

PREPARATION:

- Materials needed: Bible, paper, and pen
- Time required: 15–20 minutes

PROCEDURE:

1. Write your own epistle. It must be written to a present-day church or Christian (but don't include real names). The epistle must have a greeting, a prayer, the body of the letter, and a farewell. The body of the letter should identify a pressing issue for the church today and offer relevant advice. You may use the New Testament epistles as models, but do not copy them.
2. You have 10–15 minutes to work independently.
3. Participate in the survey to see which issues were most often addressed.

CH 11

Chapter 11.5–11.6

DISCUSSION QUESTIONS

1. List three major events in Christian history. Why are they significant? [11.5]

2. Why is it important to study church history? [11.5]

3. How does sin affect humans' relationship with God? [11.6]

4. What is justification, and how does it restore our relationship with God? [11.6]

5. What benefits do we receive when we become children of God? [11.6]

6. How might seeing yourself as a beloved child of God change the way that you think about him? [11.6]

Activity

FIND YOUR MATCH

OBJECTIVE:

You will read and discuss Bible verses to reinforce the concept of justification by faith in Christ.

PREPARATION:

- Materials needed: TR 11.3A
- Time required: 15–20 minutes

PROCEDURE:

1. Your teacher will divide your class into two groups, Group A and Group B. If you are in Group A, draw a piece of paper from the Group A bag your teacher prepared. If you are in Group B, draw a piece of paper from the Group B bag.
2. Read the half verse. Then find the student with the matching verse. If you are in Group A, locate your partner in Group B.
3. When everyone has found their partner, line up with your partner. In A-B order. Read your verse aloud in turn. Listen as your classmates read their verses and be prepared to share an observation on how that verse informs us on the concept of justification.
4. After all the verses have been read, participate in the class discussion on how being justified makes you feel. Did any specific verse have a personal impact on you?

CH 11

Chapter 11.7–11.8

DISCUSSION QUESTIONS

1. Paul wrote: "I do not understand my own actions. . . . I have the desire to do what is right, but not the ability to carry it out. For I do not do the good I want, but the evil I do not want is what I keep on doing" (Romans 7:15, 18–19). Can you relate? Why is it often hard to do what is good, even when we want to do it? [11.7]

2. When does Scripture say that salvation happens? [11.7]

3. What is sanctification, and how does it occur? [11.7]

4. What does it mean to forgive someone? Why was forgiveness important to Jesus? [11.8]

5. Think about a strained or difficult relationship in your life. How might the good news of reconciliation with God help you reconcile with that person? [11.8]

Activity

RESTORATION ROUNDUP

OBJECTIVE:

You will create a collection of tips for restoring relationships and offer encouraging words to your classmates.

PREPARATION:

- Materials needed: two containers, paper slips, and pen
- Time required: 15–20 minutes

PROCEDURE:

1. The class will form two groups. Your teacher will provide each group with a container and one slip of paper per student. Write your name on the slip of paper, fold it, and put it in the container.
2. On the board, your teacher will write the heading *How to Have Restored Relationships.*
3. When it is your turn, offer your teacher a tip to write on the board on how to reconcile or restore relationships. Then draw a slip of paper from the other group's container.
4. When all students have offered a tip, your teacher will lead a discussion on the tips that were written on the board.
5. After the discussion, write a compliment or encouraging word for the student whose name is on your slip. Then deliver your slip.

CH 11

Chapter 11.9–11.10

DISCUSSION QUESTIONS

1. Is caring for creation a distraction from the gospel? Why or why not? [11.9]

2. What are some things you can do to be more aware of and grateful for the natural world? [11.9]

3. "Redemption saves us *for* life on Earth, not *from* it." What do you think this means? [11.9]

4. Recognizing that there is no perfect church, what has been your experience in the church? [11.10]

5. Why is church community important for believers? [11.10]

Activity

GREEN GLOSSARY

OBJECTIVE:

You will assess your environmental awareness and research terms you are not familiar with.

PREPARATION:

- Materials needed: TR 11.5A, computer and pen
- Time required: 20–25 minutes

PROCEDURE:

1. Work with a partner and read the terms on TR 11.5A Green Glossary.
2. Discuss which terms you are familiar with. Then research the meaning of the terms you do not know. Write the definition by those terms.
3. As a class, discuss how these terms relate to the topic of restored relationship with creation.

CH 11 11.9–11.10 *(continued)*

Activity

THE IDEAL CHURCH

OBJECTIVE:

You will create a profile of your idea for an ideal church.

PREPARATION:

- Materials needed: PS 11.6A, TR 11.6A, paper, and pen
- Time required: 45–50 minutes

PROCEDURE:

1. Your teacher will display PS 11.6A The Ideal Church, assigning students to take turns reading the slides.
2. Complete the Ideal Church Profile in TR 11.6A.
3. Your teacher will divide the class into three groups. Obtain one copy of TR 11.6A Ideal Church Profile for your group. Compare your answers on the Ideal Church Profile to others' answers in your group. Work together to agree upon what should be on your group's ideal church profile. Include the number of staff and volunteer positions a church should have and what the requirements and responsibilities are for each position. Complete TR 11.6A as your group makes its decisions.
4. Present your group's ideal church profile to the class. Then participate in class discussion as your teacher leads.

Videos

DISCUSSION QUESTIONS

Read the discussion questions before each video is played so that you know what to listen for.

Video 1: How Does Christianity Truly Fulfill Our Humanity?

1. The speaker says the gospel goes further than just redemption. What else does he say the gospel does?

2. How does the speaker describe the internal compass he says all human beings have?

3. What longings does the speaker believe are addressed by the gospel?

4. The speaker quotes C. S. Lewis, who said that our Lord finds our desires are not too strong, but too weak. What did Lewis mean?

Video 2: What Is Discipleship?

1. What is a disciple?

2. When someone disciples us, what are they doing?

3. How is sharing the gospel different from discipleship?

Video 3: Is Discipleship More than Mentoring?

1. How are discipling and mentoring similar? What is one difference?

CH 11

Videos *(continued)*

2. What is a second difference between mentoring and discipling?

3. What is a third difference between mentoring and discipling?

Video 4: What Is a Christian's Role in Evangelism?

1. According to many Christians, who is involved in evangelism?

2. Why does the speaker believe normal people should evangelize?

3. What styles of evangelism did the speaker describe?

4. What does this variety of styles imply about how God made you?

Video 5: Why Is Church Important?

1. Why is the church important?

2. Ephesians 4:11–12 talks about apostles, prophets, pastors, teachers, and evangelists. What do these church office holders do for God's people?

3. The speaker said that the church is valuable in a corporate sense and in an individual sense. What did he mean?

Activity

HOW CHRISTIANITY GREW

OBJECTIVE:

You will research how Christianity grew and spread around the world.

PREPARATION:

- Materials needed: computer, paper, and pen
- Time required: 20–30 minutes

PROCEDURE:

1. Your teacher will divide the class into six groups to represent each continent (except for Antarctica):
   - Group 1: Asia—Adoniram Judson in Myanmar
   - Group 2: Africa—David Livingstone in Zambia
   - Group 3: Australia—Richard Johnson
   - Group 4: North America—Juvenaly in Alaska
   - Group 5: South America—Huguenots in Brazil
   - Group 6: Europe—Olaf Tryggvason, King Olaf I of Norway in Iceland
2. With your group, use computers to research the story of how Christianity spread within your assigned country or state and how the name you were provided relates to that story of Christianity. You have up to 15 minutes for this task.
3. Share your findings with the class.

CH 11

Chapter 11 Review

Take notes during the slide presentation.

Chapter 11 Study Guide

Key Terms
church
Great Commission
Pentecost
justification
sanctification

Key Verses
Matthew 28:18–20
John 13:34–35
Acts 2:1–4
1 Corinthians 12:12–14
1 Peter 2:9

1. What did Jesus mean when he said, "The kingdom of God is at hand" (Mark 1:15)?

2. How is the kingdom of God something that is already here on Earth, but not yet fully realized? Explain.

3. Explain what the church is and what it has to do with the Great Commission.

4. What is Pentecost, and what happened on Pentecost?

5. How does the Bible describe the early church?

6. What did the leaders of the Jews do when they saw the church grow? Who were Stephen and Saul?

CH 11

Study Guide *(continued)*

7. How did the church grow beyond Jerusalem?

8. What challenges did the early church have because its members came from both Jewish and Gentile cultures?

9. What additional challenges were addressed in the epistles?

10. What difference does it make that the epistles were not written directly to us, even though as Scripture, they are for us?

11. Summarize the history of the church from the first century until today.

12. How do humans relate to God because of sin?

13. What is justification, and what happens to us when we are justified?

14. In what ways does God restore our relationship with ourselves?

15. In what ways does God restore our relationships with other people?

16. In what ways does God restore our relationship with creation?

17. Why do individual Christians need the church?

18. Read and study the five Key Verses listed at the top of the study guide.

12

Act 6: Restoration Accomplished—New Creation

Act 6: Restoration Accomplished—New Creation

Chapter 12 Syllabus

Lesson		Assignment		Page
1	In Class	REVIEW	Chapter 11 Test	
	In Class	DISCUSS	Questions for Chapter 12.1–12.2	224
	In Class	EXPLORE	Activity: Restoring Hope	225
	At Home	READ	Chapter 12.3–12.4	ST 165–167
	At Home	ANSWER	Questions for Chapter 12.3–12.4	226–227
2	In Class	DISCUSS	Questions for Chapter 12.3–12.4	
	In Class	EXPLORE	Activity: Biblical Symbolism	227
	At Home	READ	Chapter 12.5–12.6	ST 168–170
	At Home	ANSWER	Questions for Chapter 12.5–12.6	228–229
3	In Class	DISCUSS	Questions for Chapter 12.5–12.6	
	In Class	EXPLORE	Activity: God's Character Bible Study	229
	At Home	READ	Chapter 12.7–12.8	ST 170–172
	At Home	ANSWER	Questions for Chapter 12.7–12.8	230
4	In Class	DISCUSS	Questions for Chapter 12.7–12.8	
	In Class	EXPLORE	Activity: Detecting Deception	231
	At Home	READ	Chapter 12.9–12.10	ST 172–175
	At Home	ANSWER	Questions for Chapter 12.9–12.10	232
5	In Class	DISCUSS	Questions for Chapter 12.9–12.10	
	In Class	EXPLORE	Activity: Face-to-Face	233
6	In Class	EXPLORE	Activity: God's Big Story	
7	In Class	WATCH	Videos	
	In Class	ANSWER	Video Questions	234–236
	In Class	DISCUSS	Video Questions	
8	In Class	EXPLORE	Activity: Patient in Suffering	237
	In Class	REVIEW FOR	Chapter 12 Test	238
9	In Class	STUDY FOR	Chapter 12 Test	
	In Class	ANSWER	Study Guide Questions	239–241
10	In Class	TAKE	Chapter 12 Test	
	At Home	READ	Chapter 13.1–13.2	ST 176–178
	At Home	ANSWER	Questions for Chapter 13.1–13.2	244

*Student Textbook (ST) Student Manual (SM)

CH 12

Chapter 12.1–12.2

DISCUSSION QUESTIONS

1. What does the word *restoration* mean? Why is it a significant word to use about the new creation? [12.1]

2. What does the word *apocalypse* mean? What is apocalyptic literature, and what is its purpose? [12.2]

3. How is Revelation like a prophecy? [12.2]

4. Describe the historical context in which the book of Revelation was written. What similarities do you see between Roman culture and your culture today? [12.2]

Activity

RESTORING HOPE

OBJECTIVE:

You will develop ideas for applying Christian hope to your daily life.

PREPARATION:

- Materials Needed: Bible, paper, and pen
- Time required: 15–20 minutes

PROCEDURE:

1. Work with your group to analyze the two biblical passages assigned to you from the list below. Brainstorm how you can apply your verses to restoring hope in your families or communities as you wait for God to finally restore all things.
   - 2 Corinthians 1:3–4
   - 2 Corinthians 10:3–5
   - Philippians 2:3–4
   - Colossians 3:12–13
   - Colossians 3:23–24
   - James 1:27
   - 1 Peter 1:14–17
   - 1 Peter 2:11–12
2. Be prepared to discuss your idea(s) with the class.

CH 12

Chapter 12.3–12.4

DISCUSSION QUESTIONS

1. What are the key images in the book of Revelation? [12.3]

2. What do the images of Jesus as the Lion of Judah and as the slaughtered Lamb communicate about how Jesus conquers evil? [12.3]

3. What is the primary way Christians follow the Lamb in the book of Revelation? What does this mean for Christians today? [12.3]

4. If God is on the throne as the true Ruler of the universe, how should we relate to the nation in which we live? [12.3]

5. What does Babylon stand for in Revelation? [12.4]

6. Do you think God can bring judgment and still be considered loving? Why or why not? [12.4]

Activity

BIBLICAL SYMBOLISM

OBJECTIVE:
You will analyze the symbolism used in Revelation.

PREPARATION:
- Materials needed: TR 12.2A and pen
- Time required: 15–20 minutes

PROCEDURE:
1. Read the directions for TR 12.2A Biblical Symbolism. Write the letters representing the symbols in the blanks next to the correct imagery from the Old Testament and Revelation.
2. Discuss the answers with your class. If time allows, talk about why you think that God sometimes used symbolic images or numbers in the Bible to communicate specific concepts.

CH 12

Chapter 12.5–12.6

DISCUSSION QUESTIONS

1. What is the biblical view of hell? [12.5]

2. Do you think the images of hellfire are literal or symbolic? Explain. [12.5]

3. Does God send people to hell? Explain. [12.5]

4. What is heaven? Are there any significant differences between how you previously thought about heaven and how the Bible presents it? [12.6]

5. What's wrong with seeing heaven as the only goal of the Christian life? [12.6]

Activity

GOD'S CHARACTER BIBLE STUDY

OBJECTIVE:

You will conduct a biblical study to resolve skeptical criticisms of God's character.

PREPARATION:

- Materials needed: TR 12.3A, Bible, and pen
- Time required: 25–30 minutes

PROCEDURE:

1. Many skeptics and even some Christians become confused by attributes of God that seem contradictory when seen through the lens of a secular or postmodern worldview. But if God's big story and the Bible's teachings about God's role and character are taken into account, this tension can be resolved.
2. Read the directions for TR 12.3A Biblical Application and complete the exercises. The three steps will help you analyze what the Bible says about God's love and justice. You should be able to articulate what the Bible says about God's character and defend the biblical view of God's justice.
3. Be prepared to discuss your answers.

CH 12

Chapter 12.7–12.8

DISCUSSION QUESTIONS

1. How does the second coming relate to believers being called *the bride of Christ?* [12.7]

2. How should we live now as we await Jesus' second coming? [12.7]

3. How are Genesis 1–3 and Revelation 20–22 similar? What significant differences do you see? [12.8]

4. Describe the new creation. Is it a discarding of the original creation or a renewal of it? [12.8]

Activity

DETECTING DECEPTION

OBJECTIVE:

You will analyze deceptive or false claims about Jesus' second coming.

PREPARATION:

- Materials needed: TR 12.4A, computer, paper, and pen
- Time required: 25–30 minutes

PROCEDURE:

1. Work with your group to read the Bible passage assigned to you from TR 12.4A Detecting Deception. Complete the research and discuss the prompt.
2. Present your group's research and answer to the primary question to the class.

CH 12 Chapter 12.9–12.10

DISCUSSION QUESTIONS

1. Why isn't there a temple in the New Jerusalem? [12.9]

2. Which aspect of the New Jerusalem are you most anticipating? [12.9]

3. What makes the biblical metanarrative unique in contrast to other worldviews? [12.10]

4. Think about the biblical metanarrative that we have explored in Chapters 6–12. How would you summarize the great biblical story? [12.10]

Activity

FACE-TO-FACE

OBJECTIVE:

You will connect key features of the creation narrative with characteristics of the new creation.

PREPARATION:

- Materials needed: TR 12.5A
- Time required: 20–25 minutes

PROCEDURE:

1. You will be assigned to one of two groups: Genesis or Revelation. Read the strip of paper given to you from TR 12.5A Face-to-Face. Genesis strips contain statements about the original creation that match with Revelation strips containing statements about the new creation.
2. With your group, form a line facing the opposite group. Stand at least an arm's length away from the students next to you. If your group is asking the questions, ask the student facing you up to three yes-or-no questions about that student's statement. For example, "Does your statement mention Satan?" or "Does your statement talk about walking with God?" You will have one minute to ask your questions.
3. If you are the responding student, answer *yes* or *no* to the questions. If the answer to most questions is *yes,* compare statements with the student opposite you to see if the numbers on your strips match (i.e. *G12* would match *R12*). Pair up if they do. If they don't, at your teacher's cue, change places with the student on your left so that you are facing a different student in the opposite line. If you asked questions during the previous round, you will answer questions during this round.
4. Once you have found your match, arrange yourselves in order from the pair with the paper containing the earliest verse from Genesis (G1) to the pair with the latest verse from Genesis. Then, each pair will read their Genesis and Revelation statements aloud, starting with the pair that has Genesis 1:1.

CH 12

Videos

DISCUSSION QUESTIONS

Read the discussion questions before each video is played so that you know what to listen for.

Video 1: Why Would God Allow a Place Like Hell?

1. Why would God allow a place like hell?

2. Why does God send people who don't want him to hell?

3. Does everyone want to go to heaven? Why or why not?

4. How is torment different from torture?

Video 2: Does God Help Those Who Help Themselves?

1. Where is "God helps those who help themselves" found in the Bible?

2. In what way does God want to help us?

3. What kind of people does God help in this area?

Video 3: Does God Give Us More Than We Can Handle?

1. Why does God give us more than we can handle?

2. How is the cliché "God doesn't give us more than we can handle" often used?

3. What will life be like for special needs children in the New Jerusalem?

Video 4: What Is Justice?

1. Why do Christians need to think about justice?

2. How can you get started pursuing justice?

3. What is justice?

4. What is the goal of biblical justice?

Video 5: Is Beauty Real or Is It Just Personal Preference?

1. What is the problem with thinking beauty is subjective?

2. Is beauty objective or subjective ("in the eye of the beholder")?

CH 12

Videos *(continued)*

3. Where does beauty come from?

Video 6: Is Heaven a Physical Place?

1. What is the state of Christians who have already died?

2. Will the new heavens and new earth be a physical place or not?

3. What kind of bodies will we have in the new heavens and new earth?

Activity

PATIENT IN SUFFERING

OBJECTIVE

You will research the stories of Christians who have been persecuted for their faith and discover how these individuals stood firm through their hardships.

PREPARATION:

- Materials needed: computer or other reference material, paper, and pen
- Time required: 25–30 minutes

PROCEDURE:

1. You and your partner will be assigned one of the names listed below. Work together to research the story of that Christian who was either from history or modern day who suffered intense pressure, persecution, or martyrdom for their faith and obedience to Jesus. Possible Christians to study include:
   - Andrew Brunson
   - Brother Yun
   - Dietrich Bonhoeffer
   - Leah Sharibu
   - Polycarp
   - Rivka Barry
   - Bilquis Sheikh
   - John and Betty Stam
   - Esther Ahn Kim
   - Catherine of Alexandria
   - Richard Wurmbrand
   - Watchman Nee
2. Record information about what helped these Christians endure and stand firm in Christ through hardship. Some things to look for might include: particular Bible verses, singing praises, the prayers of other Christians, actively sharing the gospel even under duress, and the encouragement of other Christians.
3. Share your group's findings with the rest of the class.

CH 12

Chapter 12 Review

Take notes during the slide presentation.

Chapter 12 Study Guide

Key Terms
apocalypse
hell
heaven
second coming

Key Verses
Matthew 6:10
Acts 1:11
Romans 8:21
1 Peter 5:10
Revelation 21:5

1. Relate redemption through Jesus to the Christian hope of future restoration.

2. Explain the literary and cultural context of Revelation.

3. What is the relevance of the Lamb in the book of Revelation?

4. What is the role of suffering in the Christian life?

5. Defend the Christian view of God's final judgment.

6. What is the truth about hell?

7. What is the eternal destiny of Christians?

CH 12 Study Guide *(continued)*

8. What is the significance of the second coming, and what should Christians do while awaiting Christ's return?

9. Compare and contrast the new creation described in Revelation with the first creation in Genesis 1–3.

10. Describe the New Jerusalem.

11. What does apocalypse mean?

12. What are the two central images in the book of Revelation?

13. What is the most common role of prophets and prophetic literature?

14. What is the "way of the Lamb"?

15. What do the four horsemen of Revelation represent?

16. What does Revelation teach us about suffering?

17. What choice is part of the dignity of human beings?

18. What do the terms *kingdom of God* and *kingdom of heaven* refer to?

19. What are God's promises to Christians about suffering?

20. Read and study the five Key Verses listed at the beginning of the study guide.

13

Who God Is

Who God Is

Chapter 13 Syllabus

Lesson		Assignment		Page
1	In Class	REVIEW	Chapter 12 Test	
	In Class	DISCUSS	Questions for Chapter 13.1–13.2	244
	In Class	EXPLORE	Activity: Are All Believers in God Christians?	245
	At Home	READ	Chapter 13.3–13.4	ST 178–180
	At Home	ANSWER	Questions for Chapter 13.3–13.4	246
2	In Class	DISCUSS	Questions for Chapter 13.3–13.4	
	In Class	EXPLORE	Activity: Random or Design?	247
	At Home	READ	Chapter 13.5–13.6	ST 181–183
	At Home	ANSWER	Questions for Chapter 13.5–13.6	248–249
3	In Class	DISCUSS	Questions for Chapter 13.5–13.6	
	In Class	EXPLORE	Activity: Revealing God's Nature	249
	At Home	READ	Chapter 13.7–13.8	ST 183–185
	At Home	ANSWER	Questions for Chapter 13.7–13.8	250
4	In Class	DISCUSS	Questions for Chapter 13.7–13.8	
	In Class	EXPLORE	Activity: Defending the Trinity	251
	At Home	READ	Chapter 13.9–13.10	ST 185–187
	At Home	ANSWER	Questions for Chapter 13.9–13.10	252–253
5	In Class	DISCUSS	Questions for Chapter 13.9–13.10	
	In Class	EXPLORE	Activity: Why Worship God?	253
6	In Class	EXPLORE	Activity: Who God Is?	254
7	In Class	WATCH	Videos	
	In Class	ANSWER	Video Questions	255–257
	In Class	DISCUSS	Video Questions	
8	In Class	EXPLORE	Activity: Names of God	258–259
	In Class	REVIEW FOR	Chapter 13 Test	260
9	In Class	STUDY FOR	Chapter 13 Test	
	In Class	ANSWER	Study Guide Questions	261–263
10	In Class	TAKE	Chapter 13 Test	
	At Home	READ	Chapter 14.1–14.2	ST 188–191
	At Home	ANSWER	Questions for Chapter 14.1–14.2	266–267

*Student Textbook (ST) Student Manual (SM)

CH 13

Chapter 13.1–13.2

DISCUSSION QUESTIONS

1. What is the first thing that comes into your mind when you think about God? [13.1]

2. Consider the four categories of beliefs about God. How might believing each of these affect the way that a person lives? [13.1]

3. What is perfect being theology? Is it possible to know anything about God at all? If not, why not? If so, how can we know God? [13.2]

4. Why do you think God chose to reveal himself to us? [13.2]

Activity

ARE ALL BELIEVERS IN GOD CHRISTIANS?

OBJECTIVE:
You will conclude whether all believers in God are Christians.

PREPARATION:
- Materials needed: Bible, paper, and pen
- Time required: 20–25 minutes

PROCEDURE:
1. Discuss the following question with your group: Is there a difference between a Christian and someone who just believes in God? Take notes about your conversation.
2. Your group we will be assigned one of the following verses: Luke 18:9–14, John 3:1–5, James 2:19, and 1 John 5:3. Discuss your assigned verse in relation to the question above.
3. Choose someone from your group to read your assigned verse when your group is called upon.
4. Participate in class discussion as your teacher directs.
5. Be ready to share what you now think about the difference between a Christian and someone who just believes in God.

CH 13

Chapter 13.3–13.4

DISCUSSION QUESTIONS

1. Why is it important to say that God is self-existent? [13.3]

2. If God is pure spirit, how do you explain the fact that Jesus is God? [13.3]

3. Think about the force in the Star Wars movies. What kind of God would God be if he were a force? How does the Bible's description of God differ from the force? [13.3]

4. Why is it important that God is unchanging? [13.4]

Activity

RANDOM OR DESIGN?

OBJECTIVE:

You will examine the evidence of design and defend the position that there is a designer.

PREPARATION:

- Materials needed: pen
- Time required: 25–30 minutes

PROCEDURE:

1. You are going to observe a series of objects or patterns. Assign a score from 1–5 based on your confidence that the image was designed versus a product of random natural processes or chance. A score of one corresponds to complete confidence in lack of design, and a score of five corresponds to complete confidence in design.
2. As you observe each image, write your score next to that image number below.
3. After you have written your score for Image 1, your teacher will direct the class to stand up. As your teacher counts from 1–5, sit down when you hear the number corresponding to your score. Notice how many of your classmates were confident there was a lack of design and how many had complete confidence there was design.
4. Continue in this manner with the rest of the images, making sure you write a score for every image. Then look at your nine scores and notice any pattern in their confidence level. Discuss the answers to the questions your teacher asks.
5. Watch the video and assess whether the object is the product of natural processes and chance, or the product of intelligent design based on the criteria you just identified. What led to your conclusion? Write a conclusion about design in life and what that implies.

RANDOM OR DESIGN?

Score the images from 1–5.

1. ______ 2. ______ 3. ______ 4. ______ 5. ______ 6. ______ 7. ______ 8. ______ 9. ______

Conclusion: ____

____

____

____

CH 13

Chapter 13.5–13.6

DISCUSSION QUESTIONS

1. Why do you think that fear (reverence) of the Lord is where true knowledge starts? [13.5]

2. What does it mean to say that God is righteous? [13.5]

3. It is one thing to believe that God is love and another to experience God's love. How have you experienced God's love in your own life? [13.5]

4. What does it mean to say that God is triune? [13.6]

5. What is wrong with the analogy that compares the Trinity to an egg? [13.6]

6. What is wrong with the analogy that compares the Trinity to the three states of water? [13.6]

____

____

____

____

Activity

REVEALING GOD'S NATURE

OBJECTIVE:
You will analyze Scriptures about God's nature.

PREPARATION:
- Materials needed: Bible and pen
- Time required: 15–20 minutes

PROCEDURE:
1. Use your Bible to read the Scriptures listed below. Determine which characteristic of God—holiness, wisdom, righteousness, or love—the passage is describing. Write that characteristic on the blank line next to the verse. This is a competition, so don't discuss your thoughts with others at this time.
2. Check your answers with the answers your teacher gives. Put a checkmark next to the ones you got right. Tally up and write the number of correct answers you had.

CHARACTERISTIC OF GOD

VERSE	CHARACTERISTIC OF GOD
Psalm 147:5	____________________
1 Thessalonians 5:23	____________________
Ephesians 2:5	____________________
Habakkuk 1:13	____________________
Romans 8:33	____________________
1 Peter 5:7	____________________
Job 8:3	____________________
Isaiah 40:28	____________________
Total Correct	__________
Tiebreakers	__________

CH 13

Chapter 13.7–13.8

DISCUSSION QUESTIONS

1. Look up the verses in Chapter 13.7. How are the Father, Son, and Holy Spirit described in the Old Testament? [13.7]

2. Look up the relevant verses about the Father referenced in Chapter 13.8. How is the Father described in the New Testament? [13.8]

3. Look up the relevant verses about the Son referenced in Chapter 13.8. How is the Son described in the New Testament? [13.8]

4. Look up the relevant verses about the Spirit referenced in Chapter 13.8. How is the Spirit described in the New Testament? [13.8]

Activity

DEFENDING THE TRINITY

OBJECTIVE:

You will defend the Christian Trinity in relation to Muslim doctrine.

PREPARATION:

- Materials needed: TR 13.4A, Bible, student textbook, paper, and pen
- Time required: 20–30 minutes

PROCEDURE:

1. Take turns reading the information on TR 13.4A Muslim View of the Trinity. Discuss the differences between the Christian Trinity and the Muslim view that there is no Trinity.
2. Write a 150 to 200-word paragraph defending the Trinity—one God in three Persons. You may use your Bible, textbook, and TR 13.4A as resources.
3. If time allows, take turns reading your paragraphs to the class.

CH 13

Chapter 13.9–13.10

DISCUSSION QUESTIONS

1. How does the Trinity make a difference in how we view God? [13.9]

2. How does Jesus share the life of the Trinity with us? [13.9]

3. What difference does the Trinity make for our communities? [13.9]

4. What questions or concerns do you have about the Trinity? [13.9]

5. What should good theology ultimately lead to? [13.10]

6. What do you think about the God revealed in Scripture and discussed in this chapter? [13.10]

Activity

WHY WORSHIP GOD?

OBJECTIVE:

You will list reasons to worship God.

PREPARATION:

- Materials needed: Bible, student textbook, paper, and pen
- Time required: 15–20 minutes

PROCEDURE:

1. Work with your group to make a list of as many reasons you can think of to worship God. This is a race.
2. You may use your Bible and textbook for help. You have 10 minutes to make your lists. The goal is to end up with the most reasons that other groups do not have listed.
3. Someone from the group with the most reasons listed will read them off one by one. If another group has that same reason, all the groups are to cross it off their lists. Your teacher will make sure your answers are legitimate reasons to worship God.
4. If another group has reasons that have not been crossed off, allow someone to read those items. Groups will cross off any reasons that are duplicated.
5. Continue in this manner until all reasons have been read. The group with the most reasons that have not been crossed off wins the challenge.

CH 13

13.9–13.10 (continued)

Activity

WHO GOD IS

OBJECTIVE:

You will synthesize key terms that you have learned during this course to make a conclusion about who God is.

PREPARATION:

- Materials needed: TR 13.6A, PS 13.6A, student textbook, and pencil
- Time required: 45–50 minutes

PROCEDURE:

1. Work with your group to fill in the chart for the following key terms: Perfect Being Theory, Aseity, and Doctrine of the Trinity. Obtain a copy of TR 13.6A Chart and Word Sneak Tracker from your teacher. Appoint a Word Sneak secretary for your group who will track the words being used. Each time a word on the tracker is included as an answer on a chart, place a tally mark next to that word on the tracker. Any form of a word is acceptable. (Examples: exists, existed, existence)
2. Use your textbook as your group discusses how to complete the three charts. Each chart contains a section for the definition, characteristics, examples, and false ideas. The key terms *modalism* and *tritheism* must appear appropriately within the chart.
3. Incorporate the Word Sneak words appropriately as you write answers for each section. Try to use as many words on the tracker as you can. For example, someone might say, "Perfect being theology describes how God is infinite and perfect in love, goodness, holiness, and wisdom." Write this on the Characteristics section of the chart. The Word Sneak secretary will mark the words used on the word tracker. You may reuse words. Make a tally mark each time a word is used. Each person in the group must complete his or her own chart. Assist the secretary as needed while the words are being tracked.
4. You will have 30 minutes to complete the chart. At this time, the Word Sneak secretaries will total the number of words used by counting the tally marks and record the chart total on the Word Sneak Tracker.
5. Review and discuss the examples of answers displayed on PS 13.6A Who God Is. Your answers don't have to match exactly. However, count the number of bolded words on the slides that match the ones you used on your charts to see how well your group did.
6. Share the chart total on your group's Word Sneak Tracker when your teacher asks. The group with the most words used is the winner.
7. If time allows, discuss with the class how the information from these charts could be used to respond to someone who believes that God is distant and disengaged from humans.

Videos

DISCUSSION QUESTIONS

Read the discussion questions before each video is played so that you know what to listen for.

Video 1: Who Created God?

1. What do Christians often say about the beginning of all things?

2. How do some nonbelievers respond to that reasoning?

3. What do Christians mean when they say all things had to have a cause?

4. Why is God exempt from having to have a cause?

Video 2: Does Intelligent Design Prove that the Christian God Exists?

1. What is the benefit of intelligent design theory?

2. How does intelligent design relate to being made in the image of God?

3. What does Romans 1:20 say about people and the created world?

4. What are your thoughts on intelligent design? Do you think it is a good starting point for a conversation about a Designer/Creator? Why or why not?

CH 13 Videos *(continued)*

Video 3: What Is the Trinity?

1. What does the speaker say the Trinity is? What is another name for the Trinity?

2. What three New Testament Scriptures did the speaker use to reference the three distinct Persons of the Trinity as God?

3. In which verse did the speaker say all three distinct Persons are referenced as one?

4. Is the doctrine of the Trinity difficult for you to comprehend? Explain.

Video 4: Is Belief in the Trinity Irrational?

1. Is it irrational to believe in the doctrine of the Trinity?

2. How can you support a belief in the Trinity?

Video 5: How's Christianity Relevant to Me?

1. Why is Christianity important to believers?

2. Do the aspects of Christianity have any practical application in our lives?

3. One of the foundational concepts of Christianity is that human beings are made in the image of God. What implications does this have?

4. How are we supposed to apply that fact to our daily lives?

5. How does the image-bearing concept challenge racism?

▶ Video 6: What's a "Relationship with God"?

1. How can you have a relationship with God today?

2. The speaker noted that our relationship with God can be seen in our relationships with other people. Do others see that you have a relationship with God? How?

Activity

Activity

NAMES OF GOD

OBJECTIVE:

You will research the meanings of 12 names of God and consider how they can be included in prayer.

PREPARATION:

- Materials needed: Bible, computer, and pen
- Time required: 20–30 minutes

PROCEDURE:

1. Work with your partner. Read the 12 names of God listed on the page to the right.
2. Listen as your teacher shares some information about the name Jehovah.
3. Use your computer and Bible to research what those 12 names of God mean and find one verse where that name is used in the Bible. Write what you find in the space provided. You will have 15 minutes to research and fill in the blanks.
4. As your teacher reads each name of God, take turns volunteering to share the meaning of the name and the verse you found where the name is used.
5. Discuss how a certain name for God can be used in prayer when making specific requests. For instance, if someone is sick or having surgery, they can call upon Jehovah-Rapha for healing.

Activity

THE 12 NAMES OF GOD

The following names of God may be found in numerous places in the Bible. The meanings of names may vary according to the source used.

- Jehovah-Raah________________________

  Verse:________________________

- Jehovah-Tsidkenu ________________________

  Verse: ________________________

- Jehovah-Elohim ________________________

  Verse: ________________________

- Jehovah-Jireh ________________________

  Verse: ________________________

- Jehovah-Rapha ________________________

  Verse: ________________________

- Jehovah-Nissi________________________

  Verse: ________________________

- Jehovah-Shalom ________________________

  Verse: ________________________

- Jehovah-Shammah ________________________

  Verse: ________________________

- Jehovah-Mekoddishkem ________________________

  Verse: ________________________

- Jehovah Sabaoth ________________________

  Verse: ________________________

- El Olam ________________________

  Verse:________________________

- El Shaddai________________________

  Verse:________________________

CH 13

Chapter 13 Review

Take notes during the slide presentation.

Chapter 13 Study Guide

Key Terms
perfect being theology
aseity
doctrine of the Trinity
tritheism
modalism

Key Verses
Psalm 90:2
Isaiah 46:9–10
Jeremiah 23:23–24
Matthew 3:16–17
1 John 4:8

1. Describe the four different ways people who believe in God view who he is.

2. How does perfect being theology relate to God?

3. Is it possible to know God? Explain how he reveals himself to us.

4. How is aseity used to describe God?

5. Explain what is meant by this statement: God is spirit and is incarnate in Jesus.

6. Some people believe God is a force. Why is that not true?

7. Explain what is meant by the following attributes of God:
   Eternality:

CH 13

Study Guide (continued)

Omniscience:

Omnipotence:

Omnipresence:

Immutability:

8. What does it mean for God to be holy?

9. When we say God is wise, what does that mean?

10. Why is it good that God is righteous?

11. How is God loving?

12. Summarize the doctrine of the Trinity.

13. How are tritheism and modalism false beliefs? Be specific.

14. How does the Old Testament confirm that God is three Persons in one, not three different gods?

15. What New Testament verses support the fact that God is Father, Son, and Holy Spirit?

16. Why is the Trinity important to the Christian faith? Give three reasons.

17. Is the goal of theology merely to learn more or think more accurately about God? Explain.

18. Read and study the five Key Verses listed at the top of the study guide.

14

Who God Wants Us to Be

Who God Wants Us to Be

Chapter 14 Syllabus

Lesson		Assignment		Page
1	In Class	REVIEW	Chapter 13 Test	
	In Class	DISCUSS	Questions for Chapter 14.1–14.2	266–267
	In Class	EXPLORE	Activity: Being Human	267
	At Home	READ	Chapter 14.3–14.4	ST 191–193
	At Home	ANSWER	Questions for Chapter 14.3–14.4	268–269
2	In Class	DISCUSS	Questions for Chapter 14.3–14.4	
	In Class	EXPLORE	Activity: Glorification Study	269–270
	At Home	READ	Chapter 14.5–14.6	ST 193–195
	At Home	ANSWER	Questions for Chapter 14.5–14.6	271–272
3	In Class	DISCUSS	Questions for Chapter 14.5–14.6	
	In Class	EXPLORE	Activity: Trust Falls	272
	At Home	READ	Chapter 14.7–14.8	ST 195–197
	At Home	ANSWER	Questions for Chapter 14.7–14.8	273
4	In Class	DISCUSS	Questions for Chapter 14.7–14.8	
	In Class	EXPLORE	Activity: Hope Role Play	274
	At Home	READ	Chapter 14.9–14.10	ST 197–200
	At Home	ANSWER	Questions for Chapter 14.9–14.10	275–276
5	In Class	DISCUSS	Questions for Chapter 14.9–14.10	
	In Class	EXPLORE	Activity: Growing in Community	276–277
6	In Class	EXPLORE	Activity: Castle Squares	
7	In Class	WATCH	Videos	
	In Class	ANSWER	Video Questions	278–279
	In Class	DISCUSS	Video Questions	
8	In Class	EXPLORE	Activity: My Future Self	280–281
	In Class	REVIEW FOR	Chapter 14 Test	282
9	In Class	STUDY FOR	Chapter 14 Test	
	In Class	ANSWER	Study Guide Questions	283–285
10	In Class	TAKE	Chapter 14 Test	
	At Home	READ	Chapter 15.1–15.2	ST 201–204
	At Home	ANSWER	Questions for Chapter 15.1–15.2	288–289

*Student Textbook (ST) Student Manual (SM)

CH 14 Chapter 14.1–14.2

DISCUSSION QUESTIONS

1. According to the Bible, what are some of the defining characteristics of human beings? [14.1]

2. Why do you think God created us with limitations? [14.1]

3. Is being human a problem? Explain. [14.1]

4. Do you tend to think about Jesus more in terms of his divinity or his humanity? How do you respond to the idea that Jesus was a human being with real needs, limitations, and temptations? [14.2]

5. Why might Gentiles in Jesus' day consider the doctrine of the Incarnation foolishness? [14.2]

6. What does it mean to follow Jesus in the here and now? [14.2]

Activity

BEING HUMAN

OBJECTIVE:

You will compare various quotations about being human to Christian teaching regarding human nature.

PREPARATION:

- Materials needed: PS 14.1A
- Time required: 15–20 minutes

PROCEDURE:

1. Your teacher will display PS 14.1A Being Human. Take turns reading the first two slides.
2. Discuss the quotations on the following slides. Compare them to the Christian worldview of being human.

CH 14

Chapter 14.3–14.4

DISCUSSION QUESTIONS

1. What does it mean to become like God? What doesn't it mean? [14.3]

2. In Matthew 5:48, Jesus said to his disciples: "You therefore must be perfect, as your heavenly Father is perfect." What does this mean? [14.3]

3. What does it mean to glorify God? How did Jesus glorify God? [14.3]

4. How might we glorify God in the classroom? At home? On the sports field? What other everyday scenarios can you think of in which we can bring glory to God? [14.3]

5. What does it mean to participate in the divine life and be united to Christ? [14.4]

6. What is glorification? [14.4]

Activity

GLORIFICATION STUDY

OBJECTIVE:
You will analyze Bible verses related to the concept of glorification.

PREPARATION:
- Materials needed: Bible and pen
- Time required: 20–25 minutes

PROCEDURE:
1. Complete the Glorification Study on the next page.
2. Share your answers with the class.

14.4 Activity

Glorification Study

Glorification is the doctrine that all believers will be finally freed from sin, restored, and given new hearts in God's kingdom. Because glorification is something that will happen in the future, it is not often discussed or studied by believers with more pressing daily concerns. Look up the verses. Answer the questions.

1. Read Romans 8:28–30. Who will be glorified?

2. Read Romans 8:12–17. What are we encouraged to do before we are glorified?

3. Read Romans 8:18. What does this verse say?

4. Read Colossians 3:4, 1 Peter 5:4, and 1 John 3:2. When will believers be glorified?

5. In 1 Peter 5:4, you read that those who are glorified will receive a crown. Read 2 Timothy 4:8 and James 1:12. How is the crown described?

6. Read Philippians 3:20–21. What will happen to believers that will make them glorious?

7. Read 1 Peter 1:3–5 and Ephesians 1:11–14. In addition to a new body and a crown, what else do believers receive upon glorification? What guarantees that gift?

8. In view of the Scriptures you read, why is the doctrine of glorification important?

Chapter 14.5–14.6

DISCUSSION QUESTIONS

1. How did Jesus model a life of service? [14.5]

2. What does true humility look like? [14.5]

3. Can a servant also be a leader? Explain. [14.5]

4. What role does suffering play in the Christian life? [14.6]

CH 14

14.5–14.6 *(continued)*

5. What might it look like to suffer for Christ today? [14.6]

6. What should encourage Christians in suffering? [14.6]

Activity

TRUST FALLS

OBJECTIVE:

You will reflect on the need to rely on God and his servants in times of suffering and persecution.

PREPARATION:

- Materials needed: exercise mats
- Time required: 15–20 minutes

PROCEDURE:

1. You may volunteer to participate in the trust falls activity as a faller, a catcher or an encouraging observer. Read the following instructions and listen to your teacher's directions if you choose to participate in the trust falls:
   a. There are four catchers in each group. Catchers will pair up and face each other. Your responsibility is to catch the faller. Catchers facing each other should grasp each other's wrists, not hands, to better bear the weight of the person falling. When the catchers are ready, they should say, "Ready."
   b. The faller will cross his or her arms in front. The faller should cross his or her arms in front and should take care not to bend at the knees. When the faller is ready to fall, he or she should say, "Falling."
2. In your group, volunteers may take turns doing trust falls. Be respectful of your classmate's decision on how they choose to participate.
3. Share your reactions to this activity, relating it to your readiness to serve or to suffer for Christ.

Chapter 14.7–14.8

DISCUSSION QUESTIONS

1. What is the difference between optimism and pessimism? What is Christian hope, and how does it differ from optimism and pessimism? [14.7]

2. Explain what it means for a Christian to live in hope. [14.7]

3. Explain how Peter, Martha, and Paul grew in Christlikeness. [14.8]

4. As you reflect on your own spiritual growth, do you relate most to Peter, Martha, Paul, or Timothy? Why? [14.8]

CH 14 14.7–14.8 *(continued)*

Activity

HOPE ROLE PLAY

OBJECTIVE:
You will respond to objections to Christian hope.

PREPARATION:
- Materials needed: paper and pen
- Time required: 20–25 minutes

PROCEDURE:
1. You will work together in groups of four. Assign one of the following four roles to each person in your group: an optimist, a pessimist, a defender of Christian hope, and a critic.
2. The pessimist will speak for two minutes on the state of the church today. Then, the optimist will offer an opposing viewpoint for two minutes. The defender of Christian hope is to respond to both for two minutes. The critic is to take notes on the strengths and weaknesses of each person's arguments and presentation, and then present his or her observations.
3. Within your group, discuss the critique and how you can better present Christian hope to others in the future.
4. Share your conclusions with the class.

Chapter 14.9–14.10

DISCUSSION QUESTIONS

1. Is it possible to be a Christian alone? Why or why not? [14.9]

2. What problems did the early church face? [14.9]

3. How do the New Testament letters encourage you as you think about the problems in your own church? [14.9]

4. Why do we try to be people we are not? [14.10]

CH 14

14.9–14.10 *(continued)*

5. Who does God want us to be? [14.10]

6. What does it mean to be the bride of Christ? [14.10]

Activity

GROWING IN COMMUNITY

OBJECTIVE:

You will assess how participating in church or other Christian communities contributes to personal growth and transformation.

PREPARATION:

- Materials needed: pen
- Time required: 15–20 minutes

PROCEDURE:

1. Complete the Growing in Community questionnaire on the next page.
2. Share your answers during class discussion.

14.9 Activity

Growing in Community

Think of your church or another Christian community in which you participate (perhaps even this class). Answer the questions below.

1. How has my Christian community helped me to grow intellectually?

2. How has my Christian community helped me to grow emotionally?

3. How has my Christian community helped me to grow spiritually?

4. What talents, skills, or abilities have I discovered or developed because of my Christian community?

5. How has my Christian community helped me to relate to people of different age groups and backgrounds?

6. What has hindered my growth in my Christian community?

7. What or who has contributed the most to my growth?

8. What or who could help me grow even more in the future?

CH 14

Videos

DISCUSSION QUESTIONS

Read the discussion questions before each video is played so that you know what to listen for.

Video 1: What Does It Mean To Be Human?

1. What is sanctification?

2. In what arenas of our lives should we reflect God's image?

3. What longings do all human beings have, even if we can't articulate them?

4. What does the speaker say we should do with our longings?

Video 2: Can We Love Ourselves?

1. Jesus said, "Love your neighbor as yourself" (Matthew 22:39). In what sense does the speaker say that people love themselves?

2. How should we apply Jesus' command?

3. What does the speaker say to people who don't love themselves?

4. What does the Bible say about God's self-sacrificial love and strong affection for us?

5. How will our thoughts change as we grow in affection for ourselves and for other people?

Video 3: Can a Relationship with Christ Really Overcome Sinful Desires?

1. What does the speaker say about original sin, actual sin, and indwelling sin?

2. What does the speaker say about union with Christ and grace?

3. What are two things that liberty in Christ allows us to do?

Video 4: How Can We Change To Be More Like Christ?

1. What does the speaker say about the possibility of change?

2. What Scripture and biblical imagery does the speaker mention?

3. What do we need to think about in order to change?

4. What "golden nugget" does the speaker share?

Video 5: How Do We Discern God's Will for Our Lives?

1. What statistic does the speaker cite?

2. How does the speaker describe God's will of decree?

3. How does the speaker describe God's moral will?

Activity

My Future Self

OBJECTIVE

- You will create a profile to illustrate who you could become.

PREPARATION

- Materials needed: pen
- Time required: 20–30 minutes

PROCEDURE

1. You will work individually to create a profile illustrating who you could become. Complete the My Future Self exercise.
2. Share your answers in the class discussion.

God wants the best for you. He wants you to reach your full potential and make use of the gifts and talents he has given you to serve others. Developing a profile of who you want to be, keeping in mind who God wants you to become, can help you get there. Use the prompts to imagine your future self and what you might do to take steps in that direction.

1. Where might you be in five years? What would be ideal? Will you be in college? If so, what will you be studying? Will you be working? Do you think you might be volunteering, at home, traveling, doing missionary work, or serving in the military?

2. Where will you be living? Describe your ideal place.

3. What will your typical day look like? What might be some of your favorite things to do?

4. Who will you be spending time with in five years?

5. What talents, gifts, skills, and knowledge do you want to acquire or develop? Is there a license or professional certification you will be aiming for?

6. How do you hope to glorify God in your daily life in five years?

7. How do you envision serving others five years from now?

8. What do you think might be the most difficult and the most joyful aspects of your life five years from now?

9. What might taking up your cross daily look like then? What obstacles or limits might you face?

10. What is one step you can take now to prepare to become the person God made you to be?

CH 14

Chapter 14 Review

Take notes during the slide presentation.

Chapter 14 Study Guide

Key Terms
Docetism
glorify God
Arianism
glorification
Christian hope

Key Verses
Matthew 5:48
Matthew 16:24–25
Philippians 1:6
Philippians 2:3–4
2 Peter 1:4

1. According to Scripture, what does being human mean?

2. Why do humans have a need for God?

3. Why is it important that Jesus was fully human in addition to being fully God?

4. What did Jews and Gentiles think of the Incarnation, and how does this relate to Docetism?

5. What did Jesus mean when he commanded his disciples to "be perfect, as your heavenly Father is perfect" (Matthew 5:48)?

6. Explain what happens to our character as we follow Jesus. What are some ways we can glorify God?

CH 14

Study Guide (continued)

7. What is glorification, and when will it happen?

8. What is Arianism?

9. Why is it necessary to serve others when you follow Jesus? If you are a servant, can you be a leader?

10. What did Jesus mean when he said his followers should pick up their cross daily?

11. What advice does Scripture give to believers who suffer?

12. What is Christian hope? How does it compare to optimism or pessimism?

13. How did Peter, Martha, and Paul grow in Christlikeness?

14. Why is growing in Christlikeness something that happens in community?

15. Were the New Testament churches perfect? Explain.

16. Why does the Bible give us examples of disciples and churches that were not perfect?

17. Who does God want us to become?

18. Read and study the five Key Verses listed at the top of the study guide.

15 Walking with God

Walking with God

Chapter 15 Syllabus

Lesson		Assignment		Page
1	In Class	REVIEW	Chapter 14 Test	
	In Class	DISCUSS	Questions for Chapter 15.1–15.2	288–289
	In Class	EXPLORE	Activity: Right Turn	289
	At Home	READ	Chapter 15.3–15.4	ST 204–206
	At Home	ANSWER	Questions for Chapter 15.3–15.4	290–291
2	In Class	DISCUSS	Questions for Chapter 15.3–15.4	
	In Class	EXPLORE	Activity: Strategy for Growth	291–292
	At Home	READ	Chapter 15.5–15.6	ST 207–209
	At Home	ANSWER	Questions for Chapter 15.5–15.6	293–294
3	In Class	DISCUSS	Questions for Chapter 15.5–15.6	
	In Class	EXPLORE	Activity: Method of Prayer	294
	At Home	READ	Chapter 15.7–15.8	ST 209–212
	At Home	ANSWER	Questions for Chapter 15.7–15.8	295
4	In Class	DISCUSS	Questions for Chapter 15.7–15.8	
	In Class	EXPLORE	Activity: Counting the Cost	296
	At Home	READ	Chapter 15.9–15.10	ST 212–215
	At Home	ANSWER	Questions for Chapter 15.9–15.10	297
5	In Class	DISCUSS	Questions for Chapter 15.9–15.10	
	In Class	EXPLORE	Activity: Models for Living	298
6	In Class	EXPLORE	Activity: Category Clues	299
7	In Class	WATCH	Videos	
	In Class	ANSWER	Video Questions	300–302
	In Class	DISCUSS	Video Questions	
8	In Class	EXPLORE	Activity: Discipline Your Memory	303
	In Class	REVIEW FOR	Chapter 15 Test	304
9	In Class	STUDY FOR	Chapter 15 Test	
	In Class	ANSWER	Study Guide Questions	305–307
10	In Class	TAKE	Chapter 15 Test	
	At Home	READ	Chapter 16.1–16.2	ST 216–219
	At Home	ANSWER	Questions for Chapter 16.1–16.2	310

*Student Textbook (ST) Student Manual (SM)

CH 15 Chapter 15.1–15.2

DISCUSSION QUESTIONS

1. What is a spiritual discipline? What is the purpose of spiritual disciplines? [15.1]

2. What is the purpose of silence and solitude for Christians? How is this different from Eastern religions? [15.2]

3. What does it mean to listen to God? [15.2]

4. Why is it important to regularly practice self-examination? [15.2]

5. How can you practice these quiet disciplines? [15.2]

Activity

RIGHT TURN

OBJECTIVE:

You will examine the purpose of self-examination, confession, and repentance in the Christian life.

PREPARATION:

- Materials needed: Bible, paper, and pen
- Time required: 15-20 minutes

PROCEDURE:

1. Put a check by the Scripture reference assigned to you. Work with your group to read and discuss your assigned Bible verses.
   - Psalm 51:1–2
   - Psalm 51:3–4
   - Psalm 51:7–9
   - Psalm 51:10–12
   - Psalm 51:16–17
2. Answer the following questions as you discuss the passage. Take notes as needed.
   - What does this teach us about God?
   - What does this teach us about sin?
   - What does this teach us about self-examination, confession, and/or repentance?
   - How can we follow the psalmist's example?
3. Present your findings to the class.

CH 15

Chapter 15.3–15.4

DISCUSSION QUESTIONS

1. What are some things that make prayer difficult? [15.3]

2. What does it mean to pray without ceasing? [15.3]

3. What does the Lord's Prayer teach us about how to pray? [15.3]

4. How can our work be an act of worship? [15.4]

5. Why is God worthy of our worship? [15.4]

6. What might make worshipping God difficult? [15.4]

Activity

STRATEGY FOR GROWTH

OBJECTIVE:
You will devise a personal strategy for regular prayer, worship, Bible reading, and memorization.

PREPARATION:
- Materials needed: pen
- Time required: 15–20 minutes

PROCEDURE:
1. The key to meeting goals and forming lasting habits is to set smaller, actionable goals that help you reach the larger goal. It is also helpful to create a plan for when goals aren't quite met, in order to prevent discouragement.
2. Complete the Strategy for Growth Chart to create your personal spiritual growth strategy.
3. Share your strategies with the class.

Note: If you are using a Bible reading plan (such as reading the whole Bible or the New Testament in a year) and miss a day or so, it can be helpful to begin by reading the assigned portion for the current date as if no days were missed or to shift the dates in the reading schedule. This helps keep the momentum and prevents discouragement from having to "play catch up" on missed material.

Activity | Strategy for Growth Chart

	Prayer	Worship	Bible Reading	Memorization
What goal do you want to eventually reach in each area?				
What small change(s) can you make to begin moving toward each goal?				
How will you respond at times when you struggle to make changes or reach your goals?				

Chapter 15.5–15.6

DISCUSSION QUESTIONS

1. Why is it important for a Christian to be familiar with and memorize portions of the Bible? [15.5]

2. What is the difference between Christian meditation and Christian contemplation? [15.5]

3. Based on what you learned about new spirituality in Chapter 5, Chapter 15.2 and 15.5, how are Christian spiritual disciplines different from Eastern transcendental and new spirituality practices? [15.5]

4. Why do we need to read books written by Christians with different perspectives from our own? What about books by non-Christians? [15.6]

CH 15

15.5–15.6 *(continued)*

5. Is reading fiction a good use of time for a Christian? Explain. [15.6]

Activity

METHOD OF PRAYER

OBJECTIVE:

You will practice using *Lectio Divina* as a method for Bible study and prayer.

PREPARATION:

- Materials needed: TR 15.3A and pen
- Time required: 15–20 minutes

PROCEDURE:

1. Read the directions and complete the activity for TR 15.3A Method of Prayer.
2. Discuss your answers with the class.

Chapter 15.7–15.8

DISCUSSION QUESTIONS

1. What is the purpose of fasting? What are three types of fasts in the Bible? [15.7]

2. What is asceticism, and how could it be practiced appropriately in the modern day? [15.7]

3. What is a Christian motivation for work? [15.8]

4. How might giving money sometimes make things worse for those we are trying to help? What are some constructive ways to help the poor? [15.8]

5. What are some ways that you can practice simplicity and wise stewardship? [15.8]

Activity

COUNTING THE COST

OBJECTIVE:

You will create a bar graph to compare the value of two biblical characters' gifts and relate the results to what Jesus values most.

PREPARATION:

- Materials needed: Bible, ruler, white printer paper, and pencil
- Time required: 20–25 minutes

PROCEDURE:

1. Obtain a ruler and piece of white printer paper from your teacher. Work with a partner and read Mark 12:41–44 and John 12:1–8.
2. Use the information below to answer the questions. Then create a bar graph comparing the value of the widow's offering, the value of Mary's ointment, the average daily wage for a day laborer, and the average yearly wage for a day laborer.
   - One *denarius* was a day laborer's wage (Matthew 20:1–16).
   - On average, there were 354 days in the Jewish lunar year. Once sabbaths are subtracted, the average annual wage for a day laborer was around 300 *denari*.[1]
   - A Jewish *lepton*, known as a *widow's mite*, was worth 1⁄64 of a *denarius*.[2]

   How many *lepta* did the poor widow have? ________________

   How many *denarii* was Mary's ointment worth? ________________
3. Have your graph ready for your teacher to check. Discuss the following questions with the class.
   - Based on the bar graph you created, how substantial was the monetary difference between the widow's gift and Mary's gift to God?
   - Look again at the value difference on the chart. The widow gave all she had. The ointment Mary used was considered the very best that could be offered, and it is speculated that the ointment might have been part of Mary's inheritance or dowry.[3] Did one woman sacrifice more than the other? Why or why not?
   - What was Jesus' response to each of these women?
   - Which did Jesus value more, the amount of an offering or the condition of the giver's heart? What evidence from the passages shows this?
   - Is money itself or having money a bad thing?
   - Based on what you learned, how does God want us to give?

[1] "The Jewish Calendar," Encyclopedia Britannica, https://www.britannica.com/topic/Jewish-religious-year.

[2] "How Much Was the Widow's Mite?", Tyndale, https://www.tyndale.com/sites/tyndalebibles/how-much-was-the-widows-mite/.

[3] "What is spikenard in the Bible?", Got Questions, https://www.gotquestions.org/spikenard-in-the-Bible.html.

Chapter 15.9–15.10

DISCUSSION QUESTIONS

1. Which of these saints intrigues you the most? How can you follow them as they followed Christ? [15.9]

2. Who are some of the saints in your life, including people you know personally, who encourage you by their words or example to know Jesus more? [15.9]

3. What should you do when you feel like you aren't getting anything out of the spiritual disciplines? [15.10]

15.9–15.10 *(continued)*

Activity

MODELS FOR LIVING

OBJECTIVE:
You will research the spiritual lives of historical Christians and identify three principles that can be learned from them.

PREPARATION:
- Materials needed: computer, paper, and pen
- Time required: 25–30 minutes

PROCEDURE:
1. Write the name of the saint your teacher assigns you. Work with your partner to research basic biographical information about this saint's life and how he or she implemented spiritual disciplines.
2. Write down three principles you learned from your saint's life about following Jesus or implementing the spiritual disciplines. Consider using an acronym to remember the three principles.
3. Present your biographical description and the three principles that can be learned from the saint's life.

Amy Carmichael
Andrew Murray
Augustine of Hippo
Billy Graham
Brother Andrew
Brother Lawrence
Caspar ten Boom
Corrie ten Boom
Charles Spurgeon
Francis of Assisi
Fanny Crosby
George Washington Carver
John Bunyan
Francis A. Schaeffer
George Müller
Gladys Aylward
Luis Palau
Patrick of Ireland
Susanna Wesley
Thomas Aquinas
Yu Cidu (Dora Yu)
Zhou Enying

Activity

CATEGORY CLUES

OBJECTIVE:

You will match key concepts about spiritual disciplines with their appropriate categories.

PREPARATION:

- Materials needed: handheld whiteboard or pad of paper, marker, and eraser
- Time required: 45–50 minutes

PROCEDURE:

1. Work with your team as your teacher guides you through the activity.
2. Choose from the categories in the chart below for each clue.

CATEGORIES

- Solitude and Silence
- Further Reading
- Prayer
- Fasting and Abstinence
- Worship
- Giving, Stewardship, and Simplicity
- Reading and Memorizing Scripture
- Examples of the Saints

CH 15

Videos

DISCUSSION QUESTIONS

Read the discussion questions before each video is played so that you know what to listen for.

Video 1: Why Does God Feel Far Away?

1. What phrase describes the feeling of God being at a distance?

2. Why do we sometimes pull back from God during suffering?

3. What is our knowledge of God based on?

4. How can we respond when our feelings lead us to believe God isn't close?

Video 2: Why Should We Pray?

1. Why should we pray?

2. What is prayer not about?

3. What is prayer?

Video 3: Where Should We Begin Reading?

1. Why does the speaker work through five to ten books simultaneously?

2. What is the benefit of working through more than one book at once?

3. What book is important to read when forming a Christian worldview?

4. What are some ways to read the Bible?

5. Why should we read the perspectives of those we disagree with?

Video 4: How Should Christians Encounter Culture?

1. What are three common primary postures toward culture as Christians?

2. What should our primary posture be?

CH 15

Videos (continued)

3. Should we have boundaries in consuming culture?

4. What is Christian wisdom?

5. How should we determine which content to avoid?

Video 5: Why Do We Need to Know What We Believe?

1. What effect does adopting ideas from other worldviews have on our faith?

2. What can we do to build a biblical worldview?

3. What would happen if each Christian took ownership of thinking biblically?

Activity

DISCIPLINE YOUR MEMORY

OBJECTIVE:
You will match Bible verses with related spiritual disciplines.

PREPARATION:
- Materials needed: TR 15.8A
- Time required: 20–25 minutes

PROCEDURE:
1. Work with a partner to compete in a matching game against another team. Obtain a set of cards from TR 15.8A Discipline Your Memory. Some cards have Bible verses and others have spiritual disciplines on them. Mix up the cards and place them facedown in rows to form a square or rectangle. Your goal is to find the Bible verse that corresponds to each spiritual discipline.
2. To begin the game, choose which team will go first. One member of the first team will flip over a card and read it aloud. Then the second member of the same team will flip over a different card and read it aloud. If the cards match, you may keep that pair. Matching cards will have the same number in the upper right corner. If the cards do not match, they should be flipped back to the face down position. The second team will then follow the same procedure, attempting to find a matching pair. The game ends when all pairs have been found. The team with the most pairs at the end of the game wins.

CH 15

Chapter 15 Review

Take notes during the slide presentation.

Chapter 15 Study Guide

Key Terms
spiritual disciplines
Christian meditation
Christian contemplation
simplicity

Key Verses
Genesis 2:15
1 Thessalonians 5:17
Ephesians 4:28
Hebrews 12:1

1. Explain the purpose of spiritual disciplines.

2. What is the difference between biblical spiritual disciplines and Eastern religion transcendence practices?

3. Give examples of various approaches to prayer.

4. Explain the Lord's Prayer as a model for prayer.

5. Describe various forms of Christian worship.

6. Explain how to incorporate Christian meditation and Christian contemplation into personal Bible study.

CH 15 Study Guide *(continued)*

7. Distinguish between three different types of fasts and describe appropriate fasting.

8. Relate biblical stewardship to simplicity.

9. Explain how the stories of faithful believers can encourage Christians to grow spiritually.

10. Define the word *asceticism*.

11. Describe fasting and abstinence.

12. Define worship and explain its purpose.

13. What kind of books should Christians read?

14. Give three examples of written prayers.

15. Explain the importance of prayer and the Holy Spirit's role in prayer.

16. Why is Scripture memorization beneficial?

17. What are the steps of *Lectio Divina*?

18. Why are silence and solitude important?

19. Read and study the four Key Verses listed at the beginning of the study guide.

16

Walking with God in Community

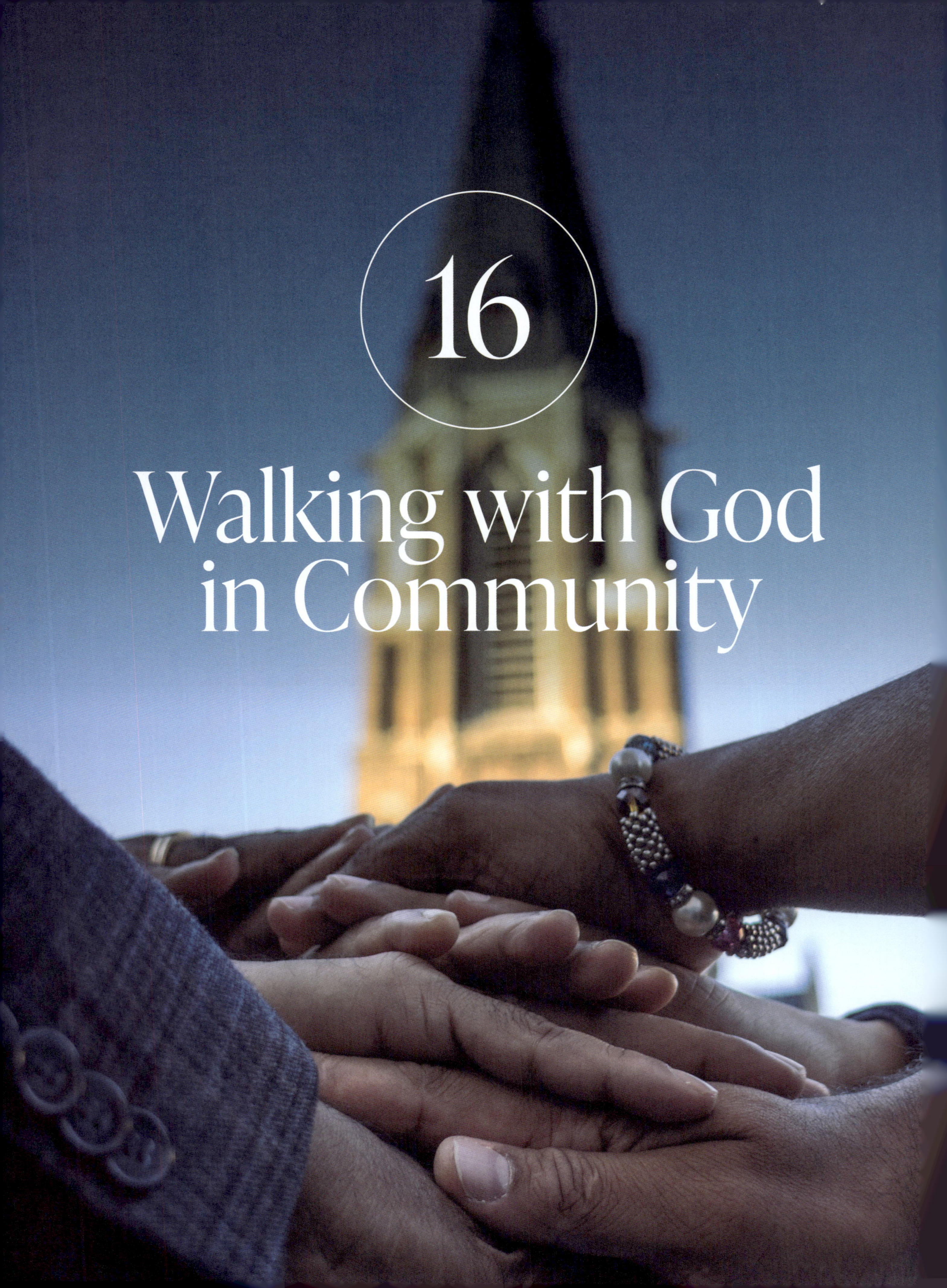

Walking with God in Community

Chapter 16 Syllabus

Lesson		Assignment		Page
1	In Class	REVIEW	Chapter 15 Test	
	In Class	DISCUSS	Questions for Chapter 16.1–16.2	310
	In Class	EXPLORE	Activity: Worship Composition	311
	At Home	READ	Chapter 16.3–16.4	ST 219–221
	At Home	ANSWER	Questions for Chapter 16.3–16.4	312
2	In Class	DISCUSS	Questions for Chapter 16.3–16.4	
	In Class	EXPLORE	Activity: Loving Church Bible Study	313
	At Home	READ	Chapter 16.5–16.6	ST 221–224
	At Home	ANSWER	Questions for Chapter 16.5–16.6	314
3	In Class	DISCUSS	Questions for Chapter 16.5–16.6	
	In Class	EXPLORE	Activity: What's the Difference?	315–317
	At Home	READ	Chapter 16.7–16.8	ST 224–226
	At Home	ANSWER	Questions for Chapter 16.7–16.8	318
4	In Class	DISCUSS	Questions for Chapter 16.7–16.8	
	In Class	EXPLORE	Activity: Go and Make Disciples	319
	At Home	READ	Chapter 16.9–16.10	ST 227–230
	At Home	ANSWER	Questions for Chapter 16.9–16.10	320–321
5	In Class	DISCUSS	Questions for Chapter 16.9–16.10	
	In Class	EXPLORE	Activity: World-Changing Words	321
6	In Class	EXPLORE	Activity: In This Together Prep	
7	In Class	WATCH	Videos	
	In Class	ANSWER	Video Questions	322–324
	In Class	DISCUSS	Video Questions	
8	In Class	EXPLORE	Activity: In This Together	325
	In Class	REVIEW FOR	Chapter 16 Test	326
9	In Class	STUDY FOR	Chapter 16 Test	
	In Class	ANSWER	Study Guide Questions	327–329
10	In Class	TAKE	Chapter 16 Test	
	At Home	READ	Chapter 17.1–17.2	ST 231–234
	At Home	ANSWER	Questions for Chapter 17.1–17.2	332

*Student Textbook (ST) Student Manual (SM)

CH 16 Chapter 16.1–16.2

DISCUSSION QUESTIONS

1. Should we imitate Simeon Stylites? Why or why not? [16.1]

2. What was the typical form of an ancient church service? [16.2]

3. Think of the symbols, banners, images, and artwork you have seen in churches. What are they meant to communicate? How could artists use their talents in the church to encourage others to worship God? [16.2]

4. What is the purpose of singing in church? [16.2]

Activity

WORSHIP COMPOSITION

OBJECTIVE:

You will create a verse of worship music.

PREPARATION:

- Materials needed: paper and pen
- Time required: 20–25 minutes

PROCEDURE:

1. Work with your group to create one verse of worship lyrics. Set it to the tune of the song assigned by your teacher. Use the theme of salvation in Christ for your lyrics.
2. Read or sing your new verse to the class.
3. Be prepared to discuss the activity with the class.

Note: In this activity, you will follow a similar process as past hymn writers, such as Martin Luther or Charles Wesley, who often set the lyrics of their hymns to tunes borrowed from other sacred or secular music.

CH 16

Chapter 16.3–16.4

DISCUSSION QUESTIONS

1. Why do we need to read and study Scripture together? [16.3]

2. Why are creeds, confessions, catechisms, and statements of faith important? [16.3]

3. What are four guidelines Scripture provides for exercising spiritual gifts? [16.4]

4. Use the spiritual gifts listed in the student textbook for reference. List and describe how five of those spiritual gifts could be used in the church. [16.4]

Activity

LOVING CHURCH BIBLE STUDY

OBJECTIVE:

You will analyze verses about love and explain how they relate to the church.

PREPARATION:

- Materials needed: TR 16.2A, Bible, and pen
- Time required: 25–30 minutes

PROCEDURE:

1. Read the instructions on TR 16.2A Loving Church Bible Study and complete the exercises.
2. Discuss your answers with the class.

CH 16

Chapter 16.5–16.6

DISCUSSION QUESTIONS

1. Why is it important to regularly confess your sins to other believers? [16.5]

2. What is a sacrament? [16.6]

3. Explain what baptism is. [16.6]

4. What is the purpose of communion? Why does confession of sin often come before communion? [16.6]

Activity

WHAT'S THE DIFFERENCE?

OBJECTIVE:

You will compare terms describing spiritual disciplines and sacraments.

PREPARATION:

- Materials needed: student textbook and pen
- Time required: 15–20 minutes

PROCEDURE:

1. Use your textbook to find the terms on the chart on the following page. Compare the descriptions of the terms noting similarities and differences. Complete the Find the Differences chart.
2. On page 317, work independently to answer the questions. You may choose to share your answers with the class as part of the class discussion.

Activity | Being a Christian

FIND THE DIFFERENCES CHART AND STUDY

	Similarities	Differences
Confession and Repentance		
Accountability Partner and Spiritual Mentor		
Communion and Baptism		

ANSWER THE FOLLOWING QUESTIONS:

Do you practice confession and repentance from sin regularly? If not, how can you change that?

Do you have any accountability partners or spiritual mentors in my life? If so, who are they? If not, who could you ask to fill those roles?

Have you been baptized? If not, why not? When you take communion, are you in communion with God and others? If not, how can you correct this before taking communion?

When you take communion, are you in communion with God and others? If not, how can you correct this before taking communion?

CH 16 Chapter 16.7–16.8

DISCUSSION QUESTIONS

1. Where does the concept of the tithe come from? [16.7]

2. How should Christians give today? [16.7]

3. Think about your local church and community. What are some ways you and your friends could work together to serve others? [16.7]

4. What do you think about this statement: "Preach the gospel, and when necessary, use words"? Is it a good framework for evangelism? Explain. [16.8]

Activity

GO AND MAKE DISCIPLES

OBJECTIVE:

You will practice sharing the gospel with a classmate.

PREPARATION:

- Materials needed: computer
- Time required: 25–30 minutes

PROCEDURE:

1. Research a gospel-sharing method, such as Good News/Bad News, Life in 6 Words, or Romans Road.
2. Work with a partner to role play the parts of "Christian" or "unbeliever" in conversation about the gospel. The unbeliever may ask questions while the Christian explains the gospel. While sharing, the Christian is to communicate care and respect for the unbeliever and include the following concepts in the conversation:
   - God is good, and he made everything good.
   - People rejected God and his ways, which is why there is evil and suffering.
   - Everyone has broken the moral law (through actions and attitudes like lying, stealing, envy, greed, hatred, and gossip).
   - God, who is just and good, must give a penalty for evil, which means we are all in trouble.
   - God, who is merciful, paid our moral debt himself (through Jesus' death and resurrection) so that justice and mercy could be satisfied.
   - Anyone who trusts in and follows Jesus will be forgiven and receive eternal life.
3. After you have role played for five minutes, the unbeliever will have two minutes to provide feedback on what the Christian did well and what could be improved on.
4. Change partners and role play another conversation from the opposite perspective.
5. Discuss the following questions with the class.
   - Was it easy or difficult for you to share the gospel? What was easy and what was hard?
   - What were some ways that you demonstrated care or respect for the unbeliever?
   - What were some positive things that happened during the conversation?
   - What were some ways you struggled during the conversation?
   - Did anything surprise you about the conversation?
   - What might help you next time you share the gospel with someone in your life?

CH 16

Chapter 16.9–16.10

DISCUSSION QUESTIONS

1. How have Christians throughout history cared for the sick and honored women and children? [16.9]

2. Why should Christians care about promoting culture and education? [16.9]

3. What can Christians learn from Rwanda and Charleston, South Carolina about racial unity and healing? [16.9]

4. Why do you think Christians have made such a positive impact on society? [16.9]

5. What is the universal church? [16.10]

Activity

WORLD-CHANGING WORDS

OBJECTIVE:

You will relate a Bible verse to how Christianity has changed the world.

PREPARATION:

- Materials needed: TR 16.5A and pen
- Time required: 15–20 minutes

PROCEDURE:

1. Your teacher will assign you to a team and give you a slip of paper from TR 16.5A World-Changing Words with a Bible verse on it. Read the Bible verse(s) given to you.
2. Keep your pen on your desk in front of you. When your teacher says the category related to your verse, grab your pen, and raise your hand as high as you can. Your teacher will call on the first person to raise his or her hand holding the pen. That person gets the opportunity to read his or her verse aloud, and in thirty seconds or less, explain how the verse relates to the category. If the verse is correctly matched to the category, that team gets one point. If the explanation of the verse's relationship to the category is correct, that team will be given an additional point. If the verse is not related to the category, no points will be awarded. The team with the most points at the end of the game wins.

   Categories:

   - Caring for the Sick and Impoverished
   - Honoring and Protecting Women and Children
   - Promoting Culture and Education
   - Pursuing Racial Unity

CH 16

Videos

DISCUSSION QUESTIONS

Read the discussion questions before each video is played so that you know what to listen for.

Video 1: How Important Is the Church as a Place?

1. What three things are necessary for church to take place?

2. What is good, healthy community?

3. What happens during worship?

4. What does mission look like?

Video 2: Is Attending Church Important?

1. Do we really need to be part of a Christian community?

2. What is the problem with having only solitude and not community as a Christian?

3. What does the church give us that we can't get from solitude?

4. If we only want to worship God alone and not in community, what does that show about our hearts?

5. What is the purpose of tapping into God's love?

Video 3: Why Doesn't the Church Address Tough Issues?

1. Why don't pastors seem to teach on tough issues often on Sunday mornings?

2. When does the church address tough issues?

3. What will happen if you approach church from a Sunday-morning-service-only mindset?

Video 4: How Does Jesus Elevate Women?

1. What was the general attitude toward women during the first century?

2. How was Jesus' treatment of women countercultural?

CH 16 Videos *(continued)*

3. What was the one necessary thing that Mary chose?

4. Why should both women and men pursue this one necessary thing?

5. How does Jesus' treatment of women contrast with first-century culture and with our culture today?

Video 5: How Can Christians Start Conversations with Nonbelievers?

1. What is the best way to start a conversation with a nonbeliever?

2. In addition to asking questions, what else should you do?

3. What will asking questions and listening lead to?

Activity

IN THIS TOGETHER

OBJECTIVE

You will give a slide presentation about living in Christian community.

PREPARATION:

- Materials needed: computer
- Time required: 25–30 minutes

PROCEDURE:

1. Take a minute to review your slide presentation with your partner.
2. With your partner, present and explain your slides to the class. Make sure to stay within the time limits set by your teacher.
3. Be prepared to answer questions about your presentation.

CH 16

Chapter 16 Review

Take notes during the slide presentation.

Chapter 16 Study Guide

Key Terms
spiritual gift
accountability partner
spiritual mentor
baptism
communion

Key Verses
Hebrews 10:25
2 Corinthians 5:17
2 Corinthians 4:16
Matthew 5:44

1. Critique Simeon Stylites' model of spiritual solitude in relation to the Christian's need to be in community.

2. What are the elements of Christian worship in community?

3. What is the value of worship services and small groups?

4. Explain the importance of prayer and the appropriate use of spiritual gifts.

5. What is the significance of confession, accountability partners, and spiritual mentors?

6. Explain the purpose of the church.

CH 16

Study Guide *(continued)*

7. Explain the purpose of baptism and communion.

8. How do giving and serving meet the needs of our community?

9. Give examples of how to share the gospel.

10. What are four specific ways the church has positively impacted society?

11. What are historical examples of the church's positive impact on society?

12. What are creeds, confessions, and catechisms?

13. What is the difference between confession and repentance?

14. What is the Holy Spirit's role in sharing the gospel?

15. What does the word *catholic* in the Nicene Creed mean?

16. List the spiritual gifts discussed in Chapter 16.

17. Read and study the four Key Verses listed at the beginning of the study guide.

17

Loving God and Others

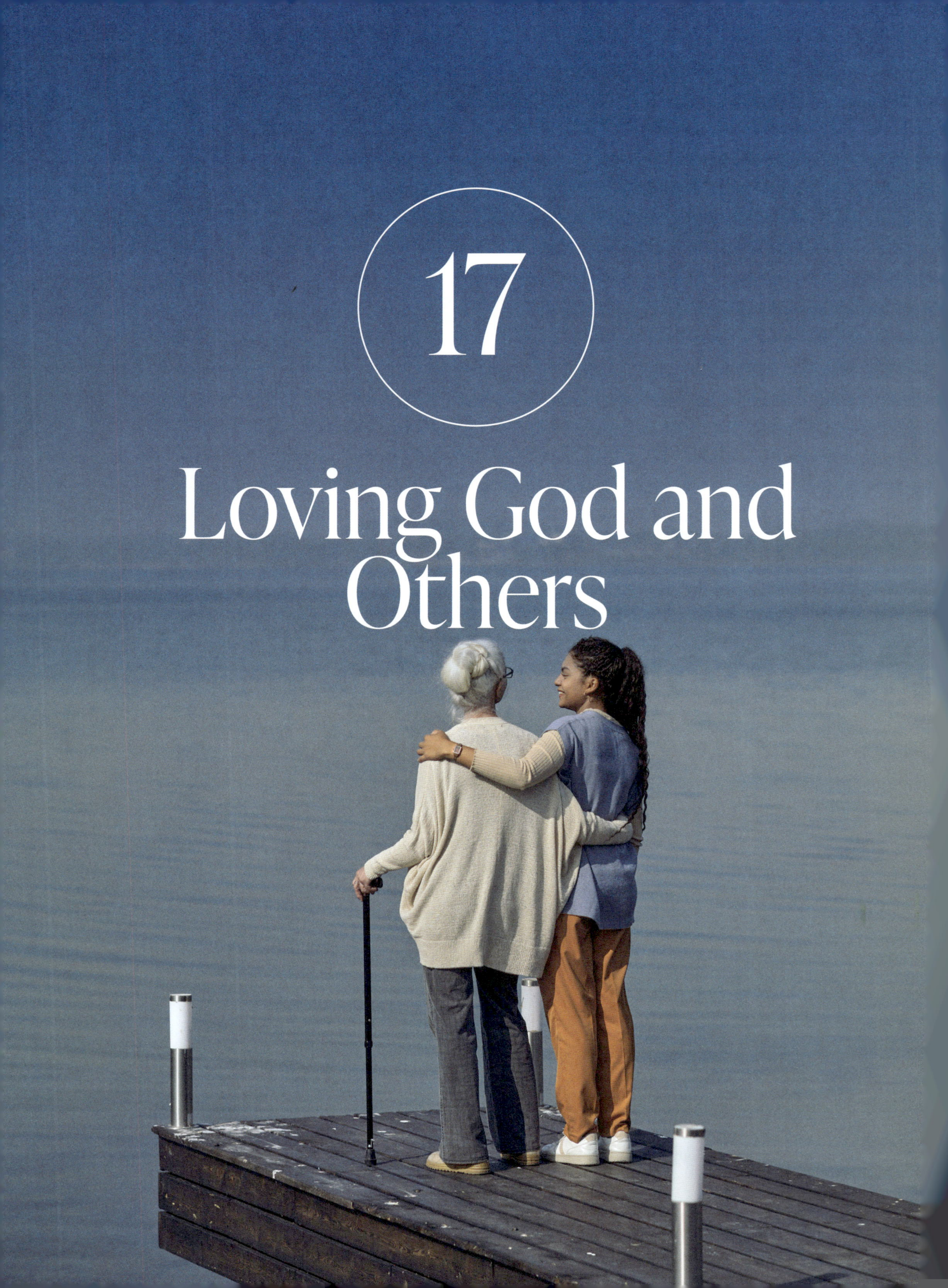

Loving God and Others

Chapter 17 Syllabus

Lesson		Assignment		Page
1	In Class	REVIEW	Chapter 16 Test	
	In Class	DISCUSS	Questions for Chapter 17.1–17.2	332
	In Class	EXPLORE	Activity: Hunting for Love	333
	At Home	READ	Chapter 17.3–17.4	ST 234–236
	At Home	ANSWER	Questions for Chapter 17.3–17.4	334
2	In Class	DISCUSS	Questions for Chapter 17.3–17.4	
	In Class	EXPLORE	Activity: Six Views on Love	335
	At Home	READ	Chapter 17.5–17.6	ST 236–239
	At Home	ANSWER	Questions for Chapter 17.5–17.6	336
3	In Class	DISCUSS	Questions for Chapter 17.5–17.6	
	In Class	EXPLORE	Activity: Ditch the Clique	337
	At Home	READ	Chapter 17.7–17.8	ST 239–241
	At Home	ANSWER	Questions for Chapter 17.7–17.8	338
4	In Class	DISCUSS	Questions for Chapter 17.7–17.8	
	In Class	EXPLORE	Activity: Good Samaritans	339
	At Home	READ	Chapter 17.9–17.10	ST 241–244
	At Home	ANSWER	Questions for Chapter 17.9–17.10	340–341
5	In Class	DISCUSS	Questions for Chapter 17.9–17.10	
	In Class	EXPLORE	Activity: Overcoming Evil with Good	341–342
6	In Class	EXPLORE	Activity: Live, Love, Collage	
7	In Class	WATCH	Videos	
	In Class	ANSWER	Video Questions	343–344
	In Class	DISCUSS	Video Questions	
8	In Class	EXPLORE	Activity: Handy Answers	345
	In Class	REVIEW FOR	Chapter 17 Test	346
9	In Class	STUDY FOR	Chapter 17 Test	
	In Class	ANSWER	Study Guide Questions	347–349
10	In Class	TAKE	Chapter 17 Test	
	At Home	READ	Chapter 18.1–18.2	ST 245–248
	At Home	ANSWER	Questions for Chapter 18.1–18.2	352

*Student Textbook (ST) Student Manual (SM)

CH 17 Chapter 17.1–17.2

DISCUSSION QUESTIONS

1. What did Jesus mean when he said that all the Law and the Prophets depend on the commandments to love God and neighbor? [17.1]

2. Why haven't humans ever been able to create the near-perfect society described in this chapter? [17.1]

3. Describe four Greek words for love. [17.2]

4. Is love a feeling or an action? Explain. [17.2]

Activity

HUNTING FOR LOVE

OBJECTIVE:

You will analyze Bible passages to determine which type of love is being demonstrated.

PREPARATION:

- Materials needed: Bible, paper, and pen
- Time required: 20–25 minutes

PROCEDURE:

1. Work with your group to search the Bible for verses or stories that serve as an example of each of these types of love: *agape, eros, phileo*, and *storge*.
2. Once your group has found the verses or stories for the types of love, show them to your teacher to review.
3. Share and discuss the different verses or stories with the class.

CH 17

Chapter 17.3–17.4

DISCUSSION QUESTIONS

1. What does it mean to love God? [17.3]

2. What is idolatry and how is it commonly practiced today? [17.3]

3. What does it mean to receive God's love for yourself? [17.4]

4. How are your current habits—your loves, loyalties, longings, and liturgies—shaping you? [17.4]

Activity

SIX VIEWS ON LOVE

OBJECTIVE:

You will contrast the biblical view of love with those of other worldviews.

PREPARATION:

- Materials needed: TR 17.2A, Bible, and pen
- Time required: 25–30 minutes

PROCEDURE:

1. Read the instructions and use your Bible to complete the activity on TR 17.2A Six Views on Love.
2. Discuss your answers with the class.

CH 17

Chapter 17.5–17.6

DISCUSSION QUESTIONS

1. What are three ways Jesus demonstrated *agape* love to others? List some specific examples. [17.5]

2. According to Leviticus 19:13–18, what responsibilities did the Israelites have toward one other? [17.6]

3. How could these standards be applied today toward loving our neighbor? [17.6]

4. What is the point of the parable of the Good Samaritan? [17.6]

5. Think about a person or a group of people that you are suspicious of, uncomfortable with, or dislike. How might seeing them as your neighbors change the way you think or talk about them? How might it change the way you treat them? [17.6]

Activity

DITCH THE CLIQUE

OBJECTIVE:

You will demonstrate the effect of cliques and prejudices on people and community.

PREPARATION:

- Materials needed: none
- Time required: 15–20 minutes

PROCEDURE:

1. Your teacher will assign you to one of three groups: Group 1, Group 2, or Group 3. Work with your group as either an "insider" or "outsider" as directed by your teacher. You will participate in one of three demonstrations to show the effects of prejudices and forming cliques.
2. For the first demonstration, the insiders in Group 1 will stand shoulder-to-shoulder in a tight circle so that it would be difficult to squeeze between them. If you are the outsider, attempt to join the group (without too much force). If you are an insider, work with your group to resist the outsider's efforts. With the class, briefly discuss the difficulty the outsider faced trying to join a group that was unfriendly and resistant.
3. For the second demonstration, the insiders in Group 2 will form a loose circle. If you are the outsider, approach the group and attempt to join. If you are an insider, work with your group to move away when the outsider approaches (no running), but eventually allow him or her to join the circle. Briefly discuss the fact that while groups were less resistant this time, one welcoming person makes joining a group easier.
4. For the final demonstration, insiders in Group 3 will form a single-file line at one end of the classroom. If you are the outsider, stand at the opposite side of the room. Insiders will stay in line and move across the room. If you are an insider, reach out your hands to invite seated students to join the line. When the group reaches the outsider's side of the room, invite him or her to join the line. If you are the outsider, accept the invitation.
5. With the class, discuss the differences between the three parts of this exercise and relate them to how people behave socially. Answer the following questions:
   - How might prejudices and cliques prevent Christians from reaching out to others (both Christian and non-Christian)?
   - How might this behavior hurt the local church?
   - How can Christians intentionally avoid or overcome a clique mentality and invite "outsiders" into community in the local church?

CH 17

Chapter 17.7–17.8

DISCUSSION QUESTIONS

1. Is it permissible for Christians to work together with non-Christians for the good of the community? Why or why not? [17.7]

2. What does it mean that Christians have dual citizenship? [17.8]

3. What are some responsibilities included in Christian dual citizenship? [17.8]

4. Nations have too often decided (in principle or in law) that a certain group or class of people is not to be considered valuable or fully human. How should Christians respond in these situations? [17.8]

Activity

GOOD SAMARITANS

OBJECTIVE:

You will discuss how Christians can respond ethically to difficult situations.

PREPARATION:

- Materials needed: Bible and computer
- Time required: 25–30 minutes

PROCEDURE:

1. Work with your group to analyze the scenario assigned by your teacher. Use a computer to research the concept associated with your assigned scenario.
   - Scenario 1: Good Samaritan laws
   - Scenario 2: bystander effect
   - Scenario 3: The consequences of sharing the gospel in a Communist country
2. Read your assigned scenario. Then read Mark 12:17; Acts 5:25–29, and James 1:5, 4:17 with your group. Using these verses or other principles from Chapter 17, discuss how Christians can respond ethically to the scenario assigned to you.
3. Present your conclusions to the class. Explain how the Bible verses you read or the principles in Chapter 17 could apply to the scenario.

CH 17

Chapter 17.9–17.10

DISCUSSION QUESTIONS

1. What are five principles for loving your enemies? [17.9]

2. How could you put each principle into practice? [17.9]

3. Why is Jesus' command to love and forgive our enemies difficult to follow? [17.9]

4. Based on what you have learned in this and previous chapters, what are some defining characteristics of a Christian? [17.10]

5. How can we cultivate lives characterized by *agape* love? [17.10]

Activity

OVERCOMING EVIL WITH GOOD

OBJECTIVE:

You will evaluate how biblical characters responded to their enemies.

PREPARATION:

- Materials needed: Bible and pen
- Time required: 20–25 minutes

PROCEDURE:

1. Work with your group to read the passages associated with the topic assigned by your teacher.

   Circle the topic assigned to you:

   - David and Saul (1 Samuel 18:5–11, 23:14, 24:2–10)
   - Joseph and his brothers (Genesis 37:2, 17–28, 42:6–8, 23, 44:1–14, 18, 30–33; 45:1–8, 50:15–21)
   - Rahab and the spies (Joshua 2:1–16, 6:16–25)
   - Sarah and Hagar (Genesis 15:1–6, 16:1–16, 17:15–21, 21:1–13, 17–18)
2. Evaluate the passages you read. Complete the Overcoming Evil with Good Study on the next page.
3. Present your answers to the class.

TR 17.5A | Overcoming Evil with Good Study

1. Who was the enemy of the story's main character?

2. Do you think the main character responded to the enemy well? Explain in detail.

3. What can Christians learn about loving and forgiving enemies from this situation?

Videos

DISCUSSION QUESTIONS

Read the discussion questions before each video is played so that you know what to listen for.

Video 1: Does God Command Love?

1. How can the whole law be summarized?

2. What are the two sides of love?

3. Should we love even if we don't want to?

4. What can the practice and discipline of love lead to?

Video 2: What Does It Mean to Steward Our Role as Citizens?

1. Who is called to steward their role as citizens?

2. What roles contribute to the flourishing of individuals?

3. How should we express our perspectives?

Video 3: Why Is It Important for Christians to Think about Politics?

1. Why is it important to think about politics?

2. What are the practical implications of politics?

3. What three types of Christian principles help us think clearly about politics and love our neighbors?

CH 17

Videos (continued)

Video 4: The Danger of Christian Clichés

1. What is a pastorism?

2. What is the correct understanding of "God turned his back on Jesus"?

3. What is a potential problem with "God turned his back on Jesus"?

4. What balance does the phrase "love the sinner, hate the sin" need?

5. How is the phrase "people don't care how much you know until they know how much you care" sometimes misused?

Video 5: What's Wrong with Loving the Sinner, Hating the Sin?

1. How do unbelievers feel when they hear, "I love you, but I hate your sin"?

2. What worldview issue makes this common saying hurtful to unbelievers?

3. What is the alternative to saying, "love the sinner, hate the sin"?

Activity

HANDY ANSWERS

OBJECTIVE:

You will identify the correct definition or description for key concepts.

PREPARATION:

- Materials needed: TR 17.8A and blue and red construction paper
- Time required: 25–30 minutes

PROCEDURE:

1. Work with your assigned team. You will be given one red and one blue paper square. Hold the blue paper in one hand and the red paper in the other. During the activity, raise one or both colored papers to indicate your answers to questions in the slide presentation. If none of the answers are correct, put your hands on your hips.
2. Choose a person on your team to keep score using TR 17.8A Handy Answers Score Sheet. Space for each question's score is provided under its designator, which consists of a Q and the corresponding question number from the slide presentation. (For example, Question 3 is designated as Q3 on the score sheet.) For each question, record one point for each team member who answers the question correctly. At the end of each round, the score keeper will add up the team's total from the round.
3. When a question is displayed, indicate your answer in 20 seconds or less. After the answer slide is shown, if you have the correct answer, keep your colored paper(s) raised or your hands on your hips until the score keeper can count the number of team members who answered correctly.
4. When the activity ends, tell your teacher your team's scores for each round. If your team wins a round, add one bonus point to your score. After all rounds have been completed, add up your total score and bonus points to determine your team's final score. Turn in your score sheets to the teacher. The team with the highest final score wins.

CH 17

Chapter 17 Review

Take notes during the slide presentation.

Chapter 17 Study Guide

Key Terms

philia
storge
eros
agape

Key Verses

Psalm 135:15–18
Matthew 5:43–45
Leviticus 19:13–18
Romans 13:8–10
John 15:12

1. What is the importance of keeping the two greatest commandments?

2. What are the four types of love discussed in this chapter? Describe each one.

3. In what ways can we love God?

4. How is receiving God's love related to the ability to love others?

5. Give examples of how Jesus demonstrated love.

6. What does it mean to love your neighbor?

CH 17 Study Guide *(continued)*

7. How can Christians contribute to building healthy communities?

8. Explain the concept of Christian dual citizenship and our responsibilities as citizens of God's kingdom.

9. Describe five principles for loving your enemies.

10. What does the Good Samaritan teach us about loving our neighbors?

11. What four questions can we ask about building strong communities?

12. What four questions can we ask to help connect our love for God with our life habits?

13. According to Luther, what three principal institutions did God ordain?

14. What is another term for institutions that supplement family, church, and government?

15. What does the term *basar* mean and why is it significant?

16. What is the primary defining mark of a Christian?

17. Why can't human beings transform society into something perfect?

18. What is the biblical view of loving ourselves?

19. Read and study the five Key Verses listed at the beginning of the study guide.

18 Conclusion

Conclusion

Chapter 18 Syllabus

Lesson		Assignment		Page
1	In Class	REVIEW	Chapter 17 Test	
	In Class	DISCUSS	Questions for Chapter 18.1–18.2	352
	In Class	EXPLORE	Activity: A Look at Jonah	353
	At Home	READ	Chapter 18.3–18.4	ST 248–250
	At Home	ANSWER	Questions for Chapter 18.3–18.4	354–355
2	In Class	DISCUSS	Questions for Chapter 18.3–18.4	
	In Class	EXPLORE	Activity: How Should I Live?	355
	At Home	READ	Chapter 18.5	ST 251-252
	At Home	ANSWER	Questions for Chapter 18.5	356
3	At Home	DISCUSS	Questions for Chapter 18.5	
	At Home	EXPLORE	Activity: Writing FAQs	357
4	In Class	PLAN	Activity: Statement of Faith Project	358
	At Home	COMPLETE	Activity: Statement of Faith Outline	
5	In Class	WRITE	Personal Statement of Faith	361
	At Home	FINALIZE	Personal Statement of Faith	
6	In Class	WATCH	Videos	
	In Class	ANSWER	Video Questions	359–360
	In Class	DISCUSS	Video Questions	
7	In Class	PRESENT	Statements of Faith	361
8	In Class	PRESENT	Statements of Faith	
	In Class	REVIEW FOR	Cumulative Test	362–363
9	In Class	STUDY FOR	Cumulative Test	
	In Class	ANSWER	Cumulative Study Guide Questions	364–371
10	In Class	TAKE	Cumulative Test	

*Student Textbook (ST) Student Manual (SM)

CH 18 Chapter 18.1–18.2

DISCUSSION QUESTIONS

1. List seven steps to reading the Bible well. Include one or two sentences to explain each step. [18.1]

2. Name the six acts and interlude of the grand narrative of Scripture. [18.1]

3. Write five sentences describing what the Bible teaches about who God is and what he is like. [18.2]

4. What does the Bible say about how human beings should relate to God? How should our relationship to God affect our behavior? [18.2]

Activity

A LOOK AT JONAH

OBJECTIVE:

You will apply what you know about the Bible's metanarrative and teachings to the book of Jonah.

PREPARATION:

- Materials needed: PS 18.1A, TR 18.1A, Bible, and pen
- Time required: 25–30 minutes

PROCEDURE:

1. Work with your group. Your teacher will assign each group a chapter of Jonah and give you the corresponding section of TR 18.1A A Look at Jonah.
2. Take turn reading the slides on PS 18.1A A Look at Jonah. Notice the questions on the last slide.
3. Read your assigned chapter from Jonah and then the additional verses listed for the chapter. The additional verses are clues to help you answer the first two questions on the slide. The answers to the last three questions are found in the chapter of Jonah that you were assigned.
4. You have up to 15 minutes to work on your answers.
5. When time is up, present your findings to the class.

CH 18

Chapter 18.3–18.4

DISCUSSION QUESTIONS

1. How does Christianity address where humans came from and who they are? [18.3]

2. What does Christianity teach about the world and its future? [18.3]

3. How do Christians answer the question: Is there a God, and if so, what is God like? [18.3]

4. How would you explain what Christians believe to someone who says that everyone has their own truth and everyone is equally right? [18.3 and 18.4]

5. What do people say about what humans are meant to do and how they should live? How does the Christian faith address these topics? [18.4]

6. Describe the Christian answer to the question: How can I know right from wrong? [18.4]

7. How do some people answer the question: What happens after I die? How would you describe the Christian answer? [18.4]

Activity

HOW SHOULD I LIVE?

OBJECTIVE:

You will compete to guess key words in verses that instruct believers on how to answer or respond to others, including nonbelievers.

PREPARATION:

- Materials needed: TR 18.2A, bag, pad of chart paper, marker, and timer
- Time required: 15–20 minutes

PROCEDURE:

1. Work with your team to play a game of drawing charades. Your teacher will choose a student from each team to be the team's timer and another student to draw a verse from TR 18.2A How Should I Live? out of the bag. The students who drew the verses from the bag will silently read their verse and sketch clues for their team to guess the underlined word in the verse. If the team guesses the word correctly, it wins a point. If the team cannot guess the word within two minutes, the sketcher must choose another student from his or her team to try to draw the underlined word or another word from the verse. The team that earns the most points wins.
2. Rules for the game:
   a. Students with the timers will set them for two minutes for every turn. Teams may not exceed two minutes per turn.
   b. For each turn, one member from each team will pick a paper from the bag and read it silently and then draw clues without speaking and without using letters or symbols. The other members of your team will try to guess the word. Team members should take turns being the sketcher.
   c. If the sketcher breaks the rules by talking or using letters or symbols, his or her team loses the turn. The paper he or she drew must be put back in the bag.
   d. A team wins a point by guessing a word correctly. Then a different team member will draw another paper from the bag and sketch clues for that new word.
3. Begin the game and play until words in all seven verses have been correctly guessed and a team has won. Each team will read the verses they won aloud.
4. Discuss what the verses teach about how believers should live their lives.

CH 18

Chapter 18.5

DISCUSSION QUESTIONS

1. What is evangelism? What does it involve? [18.5]

2. What role do good works play in evangelism? [18.5]

3. What is apologetics? What does it involve? [18.5]

Activity

WRITING FAQs

OBJECTIVE:

You will formulate frequently asked questions and answers related to Christianity.

PREPARATION:

- Materials needed: pen and paper
- Time required: 20–25 minutes

PROCEDURE:

1. Work with a partner.
2. Imagine that you have been asked to write the FAQ page for a website about the Christian worldview (an FAQ page is one that answers visitors' most frequently asked questions). Think about what visitors to the website would want to know and ask one question from the visitors' point of view. Write your question on a piece of paper.
3. Trade papers with your partners and write the answer to your partner's question. Your answer should be clearly worded, properly explain the Christian worldview, and written in a friendly and engaging way.
4. Share your FAQs and answers with the class.

CH 18

18.5 *(continued)*

Activity

STATEMENT OF FAITH PROJECT

OBJECTIVE:

You will create a personal statement of faith to reflect your understanding of the Christian worldview.

PREPARATION:

- Materials needed: Bible, computer (optional), paper, and pen
- Time required: 45–50 minutes

PROCEDURE:

1. You will work individually to write a personal statement of faith that reflects your beliefs and understanding of the Christian worldview. The statement should have 350–500 words. The statement must address the following topics:
   a. What the Bible is (discussed in your student textbook in Chapters 2–5)
   b. How sin affects the world, God's plan for redemption, and who Jesus is (Chapters 6–12)
   c. Who God is (Chapter 13)
   d. Who we are (Chapter 14)
   e. Some actions you plan to take to grow in Christ (Chapters 15–17)
   f. Your response to this information—how has this course affected you? (Chapters 1 and 18) While all topics must all be included as part of the statement, they do not have to be presented in the same order listed above.
2. Begin writing the outline for your personal statement in class and, if necessary, finish the outline at home. On Lesson 5, you will write the personal statement and finalize it at home.
3. Be prepared to present your personal statement on Lesson 7 or 8. You may either format your statement as a slide presentation (with no more than 6 slides), or simply read it from your paper.
4. If you use as a slide presentation, email it to the teacher ahead of time or print the slides to show them to the class as you give your presentation.

Videos

DISCUSSION QUESTIONS

Read the discussion questions before each video is played so that you know what to listen for.

Video 1: Does God Mostly Just Want Us to Be Happy?

1. What belief leads to today's chaotic culture? Is that belief based on the Bible?
2. What does the speaker say that God calls us to?
3. What shows maturity in our relationship with God?

Video 2: What Is Wisdom, and How Do I Get It?

1. What does the speaker wisdom is?
2. What is the first way we can develop wisdom?
3. What is the second way to develop wisdom?
4. What is the third way in grow in wisdom?
5. What is another way in which we can grow in wisdom?

Video 3: How Can We Better Understand the Bible?

1. What key practice does the speaker say we have gotten away from in the modern world?
2. How was the Bible used in the past, in contrast to today?
3. What is valuable about reading the Bible in community?

CH 18

Videos *(continued)*

Video 4: What Is the Relationship between Apologetics and the Bible?

1. What does the speaker say she wishes she would do out of obedience?

2. What did apologetics do for the speaker?

3. What does the speaker say about general and special revelation?

Video 5: What Is One Way to Reach the Next Generation with Truth?

1. What do many people believe in today's relativistic society?

2. What does 1 John 1:6 teach? What does that mean for us?

3. Jesus commands us to make disciples. What model for doing this does the speaker share?

4. What additional advice does the speaker give?

Activity

Statements of Faith Presentations

PROCEDURE

1. Take a few minutes to review your personal statement of faith.
2. When your teacher calls on you, give your presentation within the specified time limit.
3. Listen respectfully while others present their statements. Take notes as desired.

CH 18

Cumulative Review

Take notes during the slide presentation.

CH 18 Cumulative Study Guide

Key Terms

Apocrypha
canon
inspiration
inerrancy
relativism
textual variants
gnosticism
postmodernism
hermeneutics
context
metanarrative
imago Dei
transcendence
immanence
doctrine of original sin
Passover
hellenization
Incarnation
Great Commission
Pentecost
justification
sanctification
apocalypse
second coming
doctrine of the Trinity
modalism
spiritual disciplines
spiritual mentor
baptism
communion

Key Verses

Matthew 3:16–17
Matthew 28:18–20
John 13:34–35
2 Timothy 3:16–17
1 Peter 2:9

1. Explain what a worldview is and give examples of some worldviews.

2. Describe what the Bible is and how it is arranged.

3. Explain how the church recognized which books should be in the Bible.

4. Describe why relativism is a false belief.

5. Christians believe the Bible is authoritative and that internal and external evidence supports this claim. Explain the difference between the two kinds of evidence.

6. In ancient times, scribes had to copy manuscripts because there were no printing presses. How do we know that what they copied is what the Scriptures really said?

7. Explain how the creation account and Jesus' Incarnation contradict gnosticism.

8. List five common mistakes that people make in reading the Bible.

9. List seven steps to reading the Bible well.

10. What does it mean to say the Bible is a metanarrative?

CH 18 Study Guide *(continued)*

11. What is the grand story that the Bible tells? How many parts does it have? Which part are we living in now?

12. Describe three ways in which human beings bear God's image.

13. What does it mean to say that God is transcendent and immanent?

14. What were the consequences of the first sin?

15. Describe the way of Cain and the way of the Lord.

16. Summarize the story of the family that eventually became the kingdom of Israel.

17. What is the Passover? How does it foreshadow the story of Jesus?

18. Describe the history of Israel from the time of its first king to the return from exile.

19. What is a prophet? What did prophets do for Israel?

20. Daniel had a vision of four beasts. What do many scholars think the beasts represented?

CH 18 Study Guide *(continued)*

21. Was hellenization helpful or harmful to the Jewish faith?

22. Who were the Maccabees? What happened to them?

23. What factions emerged among the Jews during the second temple period? Describe them.

24. Most of the books of the Apocrypha were written during the second temple period. What purpose did they fulfill for Israel?

25. What did the Israelites expect the messiah to do? Explain whether Jesus fulfilled their expectations and his three roles as the Messiah.

26. How and what did Jesus teach about the kingdom of God?

27. What did Jesus do for us by dying on the cross and rising again?

28. Explain the relationship between the Great Commission and Pentecost.

29. Why did the disciples and early church experience persecution?
When did it end?

30. How far has the Christian faith spread from the first century until now?

CH 18 Study Guide *(continued)*

31. Apocalyptic literature conveys meaning through vivid images that are symbols and metaphors. Explain the following images in the book of Revelation: the slaughtered Lamb, the city of Babylon, and the city of New Jerusalem.

32. List attributes of God that humans do not share, even when they are made new in Christ.

33. The word Trinity is not found in the Bible. Explain how the doctrine of the Trinity is based on Scripture.

34. In what ways are believers supposed to become like Jesus?

35. Why is growing in Christlikeness something that happens in community?

36. What is the purpose of spiritual disciplines?

37. What benefits do Christians receive by participating in a church community?

38. What are the two greatest commandments, and why should we keep them?

39. What do evangelism and apologetics have to do with the Great Commission?

40. Read and study the thirty Key Terms and the five Key Verses listed at the top of the study guide.